ASHER MOISSIS

GREEK-JEWISH PATRIMONY

Edited by Raphael Moissis

Athens 2011

CONTENTS

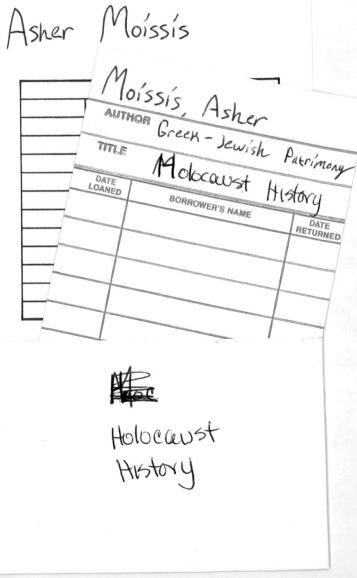

Asher Moissis

Moissis, Asher

AUTHOR Greek - Jewish Patrimony

TITLE Holocaust History

DATE LOANED	BORROWER'S NAME	DATE RETURNED

Holocaust History

Translator's Note:
Preface to the English Edition
by Alex Moissis

When David Ben-Gurion visited Greece in 1950 on one of his first trips as prime minister of the newly established state of Israel, he stayed at the house of Asher Moissis, my grandfather. Moissis (1899–1975) was a Greek Zionist leader and honorary consul of the State of Israel to Greece at the time. He played a key role during the war in coordinating the passive resistance of the Jews of Athens against the German occupiers. This resistance culminated with the kidnapping of the city's chief rabbi to prevent the entrapment of the city's Jews at the synagogue by the SS.

This book presents a collection of articles and speeches by Asher Moissis delivered during or after the German occupation and the Holocaust. They were collected in this book and edited by his son, Raphael Moissis, my father.

In them, the reader will find the heartbreaking firsthand reaction and emotions of the community leader as he addresses the surviving Jews of Athens after the liberation of the city and as the extent of the Holocaust gradually becomes apparent; a description of his face-to-face confrontation with the prime minister of the Greek occupation government in 1943 as the deportations in Salonika began, which ultimately led to the latter's resignation; and a letter to the editor of a Greek newspaper that he sent from his hideout to protest the publication of an anti-Semitic article during the occupation. Also present are his sworn statements at postwar trials of infamous Nazi criminals, including that of Adolf Eichmann in Jerusalem.

The second part of the book presents works by Asher Moissis related to Judaic, Christian, and Greek history and theology. As he sought to highlight common points of reference between the three cultures, he illustrated vividly the lifelong dilemma of the assimilated Greek Jew: his deep love for the country of his birth and its culture, where his ancestors had lived since antiquity, and his resolute dedication to his coreligionists and to the quest of establishing a Jewish homeland. A Greek heart and a Jewish mind coexisted harmoniously and flourished within him, giving rise to his extraordinary life and work.

Shortly after the book originally appeared in Greek, in my discussions with Jewish friends and colleagues in America where my family and I live, it became clear that the content would be of interest to a larger audience and in particular to those with a special interest in Jewish history. I thus undertook to translate the text into English.

The English text introduces two new chapters that did not appear in the Greek original since my father and I rediscovered these texts (in French) after the publication of the book in Athens in 2011. These relate to the immigration of Greek Jews to Palestine and to the unfortunate anti-Semitic "Campbell" incidents of 1931. Both offer my grandfather's rare eye-witness accounts of the events.

I am very grateful to Jane and John Flynn and to my wife Rebecca who were kind enough to review and comment on my translation and to the friends and colleagues who encouraged me to pursue this effort.

Alex Moissis
Portola Valley, CA
January 2012

PREFACE TO THE GREEK EDITION[1]

BY RAPHAEL MOISSIS[2]

In early 2010, I found myself, for the second time in my life, exploring the texts authored by my father Asher Moissis, in the patrimony of the archives that he passed on to me. On both occasions, the cause was my departure from a position in the Greek public administration. On the second occasion, I came to the conclusion that my father's work would interest a circle of historians, scholars, and researchers of future generations wider than our narrow circle of family and friends. Consequently, I began a process of collecting, classifying, and recording the material electronically.

Before I move to describe his literary work, and for those who may not know enough about the background of Asher Moissis, I copy here the relevant passage from *Encyclopaedia Judaica*:

MOISSIS ASHER (1899–1975), Greek author, translator, and Jewish communal leader. Born in Trikala, Moissis became a lawyer, but soon began to take an active part in Jewish communal and Zionist affairs. In 1917 he founded the Zionist monthly *Israel* which he edited for the two years of its existence. In the early 1930s he began to

---

1 The Greek edition of this book was published in Athens in November 2011 under the title Κληροδότημα. A full copy of the book with the original text in Greek can be found on the website of the Central Jewish Council of Greece: www.kis.gr.

2 Dr. Raphael Moissis has served in several senior posts in Greece's public and private sectors. These include governor of the Public Power Corporation, president of ATTIKO Metro during the design and construction of the Metro of Athens, chairman of the National Energy Council, deputy governor of the Industrial Development Bank, executive chairman of Alpha Beta Vassilopoulos Supermarkets, and CEO of Kelvinator Hellas. He is currently the executive vice chairman of the Greek Foundation for Economic and Industrial Research (IOBE) and serves on several advisory boards. In 1982 he was named Officer of the Legion of Honor by the president of France and in 2008 Commander in the Order of the Crown of the Kingdom of Belgium. Dr. Moissis received his PhD in mechanical engineering from the Massachusetts Institute of Technology, where he also taught as an assistant professor.

publish books on Jewish subjects, particularly concerned with Greco-Jewish relations through the ages. Before World War II he wrote *Dheka pende imere ana tin Evraikyin Palestinin* ("Fifteen Days Across Jewish Palestine," 1933), *Isagogyi is to Oikoyeniakon Dhikyeon ton en Elladi Israiliton* ("Introductory Study of the Civil Laws of the Jewish Family in Greece," 1934) and a translation of the *Autoemancipation* of J. L. Pinsker (1933). He was president of the Jewish National Fund (1930-1938), of the Salonika Jewish community (1934–36), and of the Greek Zionist Federation (1936–38). Following the liberation of Greece, Moissis resumed his communal and literary activities. He was president of the Central Council of Jewish Communities in Greece (1944-49) and, from 1948, the diplomatic representative of Israel in Athens. He translated parts of the diaries of Theodor Herzl (1952) and the *History of Modern Hebrew Literature* by Joseph Klausner (1968). His postwar books include *I Filia Ellinon kye Evreon ana tous Eonas* ("The Friendship of Jews and Greeks Through the Centuries," 1953), *Ellenoioudhaikye Melete* ("Helleno-Judaic Studies," 1958), and *Pion Ellinismon Katepolemisan I Makkavei* ("The Hellenism that the Maccabees Fought," 1962). After the Six-Day War of 1967 he wrote *Istoria kye Thrili yiro apo to Tikhos ton Dhakrion* ("History and Legend Concerning the Wailing Wall," 1968), which was translated into Italian and English, the latter by Rae Dalven. Moissis also translated into Greek verse the *Haggadah* (1970). Moissis was probably the most committed and prolific Jewish writer in modern Greece. [R.D.]

Additional details on the life and work of Asher Moissis were published by Steven Bowman, professor of Judaic Studies at the University of Cincinnati, in his article "The Contribution of Asher Raphael Moissis."[3] Also related is my own presentation in October 2010 at an event of the Jewish Community of Trikala.[4]

---

3 See Steven Bowman, "The Contribution of Asher Raphael Moissis," Studies in Bibliography and Booklore 12 (1979), 25–27(vol. 30, 2010) and the Chronika of the Central Jewish Council of Greece (vol. 34, 2011).

4 The full text of the speech appeared in the journals Trikalina (vol. 30, 2010) and the Chronika of the Central Jewish Council of Greece (vol. 34, 2011).

The literary work of Asher Moissis can be divided into two categories. The first contains the works that he published in books and that I will simply list here as a reference. By publication date, they are:

- *Introduction to the Family Law of the Jews in Greece* (1934, in Greek).[5] The text examines the origins and history of Jewish law and includes texts from the rabbinic codes.
- *Judaic-Greek Studies* (1959, in Greek).[6] This investigates elements from ancient and modern history with a special emphasis on common points of reference.
- Translation from Hebrew into Greek of Professor Joseph Klausner's *History of Modern Jewish Literature (1965, in Greek).*[7]
- *Day of Atonement Prayer Book* (1969, in Greek and Hebrew). Greek translation is presented alongside the original Hebrew text.[8]
- *Passover Narrative* (1971, in Greek and Hebrew). Greek translation in verse is presented alongside the original text of the Passover Haggadah with an extensive introduction.[9]
- *The Psalms of David* (1973, in Greek and Hebrew). Greek translation in verse is presented alongside the original Hebrew text.[10]

The second category of works by Asher Moissis consists of a number of speeches and articles, some published in journals, others typed, and yet others handwritten, many complete and some in draft form, along with two tape-recorded speeches. Some of the articles had been published, in their entirety or in part, in Greek newspapers, primarily the *Evraiki Estia*, where he was copublisher; most, however, had as their sole audience those who happened to attend his speech.

---

5 Εισαγωγή εις το Οικογενειακόν Δίκαιον των εν Ελλάδι Ισραηλιτών (1934).

6 Ελληνο-ιουδαϊκαί Μελέται (1959).

7 Επίτομος Ιστορία εβραϊκής λογοτεχνίας (1965).

8 Προσευχολόγιο της Ημέρας του Εξιλασμού (1969).

9 Πασχαλινή Διήγησις (1971).

10 Οι Ψαλμοί του Δαβίδ (1973).

I decided to focus on this second category of works, aspiring to organize and present them. I thought it useful to classify this rich set of materials into subject areas. I distributed them as follows:

-Holocaust
-Palestine and the State of Israel
-Religious Studies on Judaism and Christianity
-Greeks and Jews as Nations
-Others

Part one of the current collection of articles is dedicated to the Holocaust. Modern literature on the Holocaust is universal and extensive with significant historical records, testimonies from survivors of the camps, journals, original motion pictures, and even poems, novels, and plays. However, many of these were created two or three decades after the tragic events, in calmer times, and with their authors having the opportunity to do systematic historical research and make use of information gathered by then in very authoritative databases. By contrast, the texts written by Asher Moissis in part one of this book were written in the heat of the moment, with his personal recollections and those of friends serving as his sole reference. It is this characteristic of the texts that gives them historical value and excuses certain imperfections in the description of events.

In addition to the first texts and speeches delivered right after the liberation, I have included in this section material related to my father Asher Moissis' depositions in two sensational trials related to the Holocaust: the trial of German officer Max Merten, the executioner of Salonika, which took place in Athens; and the trial of the infamous Eichmann in Jerusalem. I also include a private letter in which Asher Moissis refers to acts of resistance by Greek Jews during the German occupation, along with correspondence related to the role of the chief rabbi of Salonika, Sewy Koretz.

I also include in the same section the translation of the article "Against Apion, or About the Impudence of the Jews." While the subject area for this article would belong in part two of the book, I include it here because my father wrote it while in hiding during the German occupation, and it reflects vividly his feelings at the time.

Part one also includes my own description of the rescue of our family in Kifissia from the hands of collaborators thanks to my father's quick thinking. I include it here because, while the text was not written by Asher Moissis, the exploits described are all his own.

I did not include in this collection his works on "Palestine and the State of Israel," considering these to be outdated. These consist primarily of speeches he delivered during anniversaries from the founding of the State of Israel, starting from the first anniversary in 1949 and continuing almost each year until the twenty-fifth.

In part two, I have included texts of Judaic and Christian interest; these could be considered as additions to his book *Judaic-Greek Studies*. My father had a very interesting correspondence related to this book with the Greek Orthodox Patriarch of Jerusalem Venediktos.

Finally, part three includes historical accounts by Asher Moissis, who witnessed or directly influenced these events, of the interwar immigration of Greek Jews to Palestine and the anti-Semitic "Campbell" incidents of Salonika of 1931. Also included is a note entitled "Leon Recanati and I" because it presents interesting aspects of the history of the Jewish community of Salonika in the last few years before its destruction and includes useful information on the personalities and actions of both Recanati and Asher Moissis.

The section also includes an article related to the participation of Jews in the Greek armed forces and the still very relevant speech on the "Ancient Jewish Testimonials on the Greekness of Macedonia."

The present collection closes with a text that is (unfortunately) so current and relevant to Greece's current political challenges that one can't help wondering whether it was written by Asher Moissis in 1968 or whether it was a study published in 2011!

I owe a warm thanks to my classmate and old friend Professor Dionisis Magliveras, who shared with much consideration and interest my dilemma regarding the usefulness of this publication. In the end he encouraged me, noting that many of the present texts, beyond their unquestionable historical value, remain current; furthermore, some of the subjects covered continue to be relevant today. Finally, I thank Mrs. Titika Papachristou for the innumerable hours she dedicated with care and attention to the review and correction of these texts.

Raphael Moissis
Kifissia, spring 2011

PART ONE

HOLOCAUST

AGAINST APION,
OR ABOUT THE IMPUDENCE OF THE JEWS

On August 20, 1944, the newspaper Eleftheron Vima published an awful anti-Semitic article signed by a theologian, a regular columnist named N. Nicolaides. Asher Moissis, who just a few days earlier had escaped arrest by the Germans, had the courage to draw a response entitled "Against Apion, or About the Impudence of the Jews," which paraphrases the famous apologetic in the AD first century by Flavius Josephus "Against Apion, or About the Antiquity of the Jews." The letter sent was not published in Eleftheron Vima during the Occupation but appeared one year later, on August 10, 1945, in the journal Deltion Evraikon Idiseon, which was the forerunner to the journal Evraiki Estia. The following is an exact copy of the typewritten document found among my father's papers.

"They struggle to rebuild the Temple of Jerusalem to refute the Lord. And what is it that they do not have! Money abundant, political power everywhere, impudence unimaginable, militancy indomitable. Yet the divine Power prevents and will abort conclusively the effort to rebuild His Temple in Jerusalem..."

Thus you write, Mr. Nicolaides, in the conclusion to your most recent religious article in the August 20, 1944, Sunday edition of the newspaper *To Eleftheron Vima*, which for years I have followed with interest, both for the elegant style of its content and for its deep theological meaning.

During frequent discussions with my Orthodox secular and clerical friends, the theme of the educational level of the Greek clergy and more generally of Greek theologians relative to that of their Western colleagues and, in particular, their colleagues across the ocean, I confess that I would not miss an opportunity to refer to your inspired publications to demonstrate how I understood the intellectuality and the awareness of the true role of the clergy and of theologians in Greece.

Without changing my views about you but with a desire, in fact, to keep them undisturbed, I am led to write to you from my hiding place this poorly written note to convey the beliefs of those like me regarding the issue that you touch upon with the fragment of your article that I quote and highlight above.

"...They struggle to rebuild the Temple in Jerusalem," you write.

As the learned man that you are, aware—as you must be—of our issues, you know of course that until now there has been no attempt to repair the temple, and neither was the thought for the achievement of such an objective ever manifested by those who manage our affairs and who are carriers of our ideas. By this I do not mean to say that we have waived the right to construct our temple where the best of our architects—and you know how many such famous ones we have—would deem most appropriate, even if this is to be done over the devastated and, by the tears of so many generations, soaked walls of the Ancient Temple; nor that we recognize in others the right to become involved in this internal affair of ours. However, I repeat, such an issue was neither raised to date nor discussed by anyone.

Thus, what you write about a "struggle" for the reconstruction of the temple is based on a condition totally nonexistent and imaginary. It is, however, possible that by talking about a temple you are speaking allegorically, and by the alleged rebuilding, you are hinting at our struggles for our reunification in our old and historic country and for our conclusive deliverance from the intolerable consequences of the Diaspora. If this is it, I do not hesitate to write to you that, on this point at least, you are thinking anachronistically, that your spirit has not yet been able to free itself from those old superstitions, and that you did not have the opportunity to reflect on the meaning of our contemporary struggles. How little do you know our movement and how much less our modern one to reach the bitter and unjust conclusion that "we struggle to reconstruct the Temple" and even "to deny the Lord."

Our struggles, ever since they started with the appearance in 1882 in Odessa of Leo Pinsker's Jewish *Auto-Emancipation* (my own translation to

Greek can be found in the Greek National Library[11]) and then took a specific political form with the publication a few years later of *The Jewish State* by Theodore Herzl, these struggles of ours, I say, never had a religious character. What describes and distinguishes us moderns from our ancestors is that we methodically conducted the diagnosis of our illness, and we know from what we suffer and how and where to treat it. While our unfortunate fathers thought that the nations around us were solely responsible for our misery and our suffering and kept trying in vain to find a panacea, not to cure—that would have been a dream—but only to soften and to relieve their pain, we, in contrast, believe with the most resolute and confirmed faith that the deepest cause of the canker that eats our entire flesh for centuries lies and acts through our body, in our very existence.

Thanks to the concession made to us after the French Revolution by the European nations one after another to accept us within their social circles, we were able to free ourselves from the old prejudices and abandon the strange and whimsical exclusivity of only examining and studying our religious books. And to tell the truth, the European spirit was not only not injured but, on the contrary, benefited considerably from this concession. Once we finally started to observe our problem under the magnifying glass of sociological and biological research, we arrived at the conclusion that our illness is organic and the means of its treatment should necessarily affect its very organic existence. If you had the chance to browse through our modern and fairly rich literature, written of course in our revived national language, you would see, my dear friend, how our contemporary struggles are impregnated by those ideas and how these ideas are foreign to the motives and aims that you unjustly attribute to us.

Let's switch roles for a moment and suppose that we are both living during those glorious Greek days of 1821 and that you are a member of the Greek Diaspora living in Europe, a sworn associate of the secret society Filiki Eteria, and that I am—let's say—my coreligionist Georges Laffitte, who instead, as you probably know he did, of writing fiery articles in *France Libre* in favor of the Greek case and of rousing the French public opinion to the point of

---

11 ΛΕΟΝΤΟΣ ΠΙΝΣΚΕΡ «ΑΥΤΟΧΕΙΡΑΦΕΤΗΣΙΣ» ΜΕΤΑΦΡΑΣΙΣ ΑΣ. ΜΩΥΣΗ, ΕΚΔΟΣΙΣ «ΕΒΡΑΪΚΗΣ ΑΝΑΓΕΝΝΗΣΕΩΣ» ΘΕΣΣΑΛΟΝΙΚΗ 1934

forcing Louis XVIII to come out at night to the balcony of the Tuileries Palace in his nightgown to promise to the protesting mob support for the struggling Greeks, instead of writing these articles, I, Laffitte, got caught up in a discussion, for example, on the unjust condemnation of Socrates by the ancient Greeks and wrote that the Greeks "now struggle to rebuild the Parthenon in order to transform it again into a Temple of the Olympian gods, to restore paganism, and to deny the one true God."

Do I need to rate the bitterness that you would have felt then, you the fighter of the so just Greek cause, for the great misunderstanding of your intentions and of your purpose?

As I said, our struggles have nothing whatsoever to do with those religious disputes and beliefs. But if you wish to examine the position taken by militants of these struggles and more generally by our contemporary scholarly world towards the teaching and the personality of the founder of the Christian religion, you would be convinced that this position is completely revisionist; our revised and freed from any old superstitions emancipated position tends not to "deny the Lord," as you write, but to confirm him and his teaching.

Did you by any chance read the erudite book written in modern Hebrew and translated in many European countries by the University of Jerusalem Professor Joseph Klausner, *Yeshu HaNotzri* ("Jesus of Nazareth")? Have you heard about a sensational work of the Jewish-American rabbi Enelow entitled *A Jewish View on Jesus*? What do you know about the ideas broadcast for several years on this issue in Jewish synagogues and Protestant churches by the renowned chief rabbi of New York, Stephen Wise?

If my circumstances—a state of one who is being relentlessly persecuted—allowed me to have in my hands the relevant texts and to refer you to certain citations from the opinions of the most authoritative and formal representatives of contemporary Jewish thinking regarding the founder of Christianity and his teachings, you would experience the most-unexpected surprise at the progress we have made in recent years on the issue of our position and our relations toward the by so many millions deified great son of Israel. You would find how much we are now freed from our old fanaticism and the extent to which we are now proud because we happen to belong to the race from the depths of which originated the God of the most populous perhaps and the finest—this without the *perhaps*—portion of mankind.

A document indicative of the "circumstances" that Asher Moissis describes in his letter to the editor: an official certificate, signed by the Italian and Greek authorities at the notorious Averoff prison, verifying that Asher Moissis was held at the prison from September 26 to October 8, 1942. He survived the ordeal thanks to the fact that Athens at the time was under Italian and not German occupation.[12]

If the present and the future were judged only from the perspective of the past, many of the symptoms of human life would be left without a historical and philosophical explanation. It is therefore a historical and philosophical mistake for you to want to judge our current and future directions based only on old and outdated ideas of ours, just as it is unfair to want to draw conclusions about the current aspirations of the Egyptian people by unearthing

---

12 Some additional detail on the circumstances surrounding this arrest and imprisonment of Asher Moissis can be found in a later chapter of this book, "The Participation of Jews in Resistance Activities."

their pharaonic sarcophagi and mummies. As much as it is logically inconsistent to attempt to appreciate the modern ideals of the reborn Greek nation
from the psychoanalysis of the mentality of the House of Five Hundred,
which twenty-five centuries ago issued the condemnation of the before Christ
anointed one, just as much it would be unphilosophical for us to survey the
struggles of a people trying to establish a new and more bearable life from
the pages of the Talmud and the Midrash that have faded and been covered
with the dust of centuries.

You also speak of evil designs, of impudence, etc. I would like, for truth's
sake, to ask you: how do you interpret these peculiar qualities of our race?
As innate and ingrained, like disease-causing blood cells that circulate in the
blood of our sick organism since the time perhaps of the original sin? Or as
acquired and passed on to us by the Diaspora and the persecutions?

You cannot of course think the former because you would be in danger of being characterized as guilty of blasphemy and hubris against the
founder and the first builders and advocates of the Christian religion: both
the harmless Nazarene, His disciples, and most, if not all, of the first hiero-
phants of Christendom had in their veins the same unaltered blood of our
race and, in fact, their racial characteristics were more pronounced than
ours, since they had not yet been influenced by the subsequent racial mix-
ing. By accepting, however, by necessity, the latter, namely that our race
was not evil and impudent from the beginning and still not evil, impudent,
etc., when Christianity appeared but that it ended up such after its Diaspora
and the persecutions that sociologically influenced, deformed, and—why
not?—diluted in part its true racial character, then why do you curse and
ironize our efforts to reconstitute our old, proper national life that will free
us from the causes of our alleged defects, will improve our racial character,
and will contribute to our expelling Satan and eliminating our admitted or
concealed evil plans?

As the good Christian that you are and as a profound reader of the scriptures, you know of course that the prophecies relating to the arrival of the
Savior on earth were associated with prophetic and angelic assurances that,
simultaneously with his coming, the human race would be blessed with the
prevalence of more justice, peace, and joy.

8

I, who did not happen to be born to Christian parents and who have not succeeded yet to form a definite opinion on whether Christ did once truly visit the people on earth and teach them divinely the lessons of justice, peace, and truth; I, who gaze plaintively these days at the mundane and watch people destroying one another and competing to invent V-1 retaliation arms; I, who sees my fellow countrymen persecuted and forced to work for new Pithom and Ramses in the heart of Europe to raise pyramids to neopaganism; I, threatened myself at any minute to become one such slave; as I read now the last lines of your article, I send to the heavens from the depths of my soul this simple and modest prayer:

"Sweet and sublime Nazarene, brother of my fathers, forgive me if I do not go to the churches to worship You and to pay homage to You. Whether you did or did not once come to earth, yes or no, it is certainly necessary for you to return now—in fact, as soon as possible—to reeducate people on Your Gospel. And you can be sure that, thanks to the radio, the airplane, and so many other tools that mankind discovered in the meantime, this time you will not fail."

—Flavius Josephus[13]

---

13 When he sent this letter to the newspaper editor, Asher Moissis was hiding with his family in the Kifissia suburb of Athens under the false name of Alexandros Mantzaris and with a fake identification card issued by Aggelos Evert, the chief of police in Athens. He signed the letter with the obviously false name of Flavius Josephus because he did not want to attract any further attention to himself from the occupiers. In any case, we now know that his name was already on the German "most wanted" list.

LIBERATION — THE JEWS OF GREECE MEET AGAIN

This text comes from a speech by Asher Moissis at a 1971 event to commemorate twenty-five years from the establishment of the Foundation for the Vocational Rehabilitation of Greek Jews.

On October 11, 1944—in other words, one day before the evacuation of the city of Athens by the last German forces—I and three to four coreligionists met at a café on Alexandras Avenue to exchange our first views on how we would start the reconstruction of our destroyed communal life. I read them a draft I had edited that evolved a few months later to become Law 367/1945 on the establishment of the Central Jewish Council and Law 886/1945 on the establishment of the OPAIE.[14] These pencil-written drafts I keep as souvenirs and will offer to the now under-construction Jewish Museum of Athens. The next day, October 12, 1944, after confirming that our life was no longer in danger, several Jews, almost instinctively, all headed to Melidoni Street.[15] We all looked like storm-tossed castaways. Some were all skin and bones from hunger; others, on the contrary, were swollen from the lack of vitamins, but all were shabby and with an appearance that depicted our sadness and our anguish. We conducted a first religious ceremony and sounded the sofar to invite to join us those of our brethren who had been displaced savagely by our ruthless persecutor and whose tragic fortunes we did not yet know. On this first such free Jewish gathering, we elected by acclamation a temporary committee for the administration of our urgent issues and approved a resolution of gratitude to the Greek people for their fraternal assistance and support in our rescue. The resolution was printed immediately and posted in central points of Athens.

---

14 The initials ΟΠΑΙΕ were an acronym for the Relief and Rehabilitation Agency of the Jews of Greece (Οργανισμος Περιθαλψεως και Αποκαταστασεως Ισραηλιτων Ελλαδος).

15 Melidoni Street was then and continues to be now the site of the synagogue of Athens.

RESOLUTION

We the Israelites located around the city of Athens, survivors by Divine Grace of the savage persecution of the German hordes, having just restored our free communal life following the glorious acts of the liberating Greek and Allied troops, after conveying our thanks to the Lord for our rescue from the implacable persecution declared against us, feel as our next primary task to declare publicly and before all free mankind our feelings of profound gratitude that we and our descendants will carry toward the Greek people in their entirety, who by all kinds of moral and material support and assistance made our rescue possible.

We are especially grateful to the Greek government-in-exile during the period of enemy occupation for its repeated recommendations via radio and other means to the Greek authorities and the Greek people in favor of providing us with assistance and support as well as its other actions overseas for us; to the archbishop of Athens and the entire Greek Orthodox Church for its strong position and loving care in moments very difficult for us; to the heads of the Greek political parties; to the Greek scientific institutions; to the patriotic organizations and others for the empathy, sympathy, and philanthropy they demonstrated; and especially to the authorities, officers, and men of all resistance forces for their actions in favor of those Israelites who sought refuge and who fought in the Greek mountains during the persecution.

This truly brotherly stance of the Greek people at times so critical for us increased our love and devotion to our Greek homeland where we have lived over so many generations in undisturbed harmony and makes us eager to make every sacrifice for its well-being and its magnificence.

—THE TEMPORARY CENTRAL
COUNCIL OF THE JEWISH COMMUNITIES OF GREECE

Liberation Speech: "Get Strong and Be Brave"
(ΕΡΡΩΣΘΕ ΚΑΙ ΑΝΔΡΙΖΕΣΘΕ)

This speech was delivered by Asher Moissis at the first event following the liberation of Athens in October 1944. While Greece itself was free, the war in Europe against Germany would continue for over six months until the fall of Berlin in May 1945. At the time of the speech, the concentration camps and the crematoriums in Poland and elsewhere were still operating and the Jewish Holocaust still underway. The speech reflects the raw emotions of the survivors against the former occupiers and the lingering hope, which was to be so devastatingly dashed, that the exiled Jews of Greece would one day return. It also reflects the Zionist leader's combined love for his religious brothers and tradition and for the inhabitants and culture of his country of birth. An interesting characteristic of the Holocaust of the Jews in Greece is that it occurred in two primary waves that were separated by one year: the first wave occurred in 1943 for Salonika and those provinces of the country, mostly in the north, that were occupied by the Germans and the Bulgarians, and the second wave occurred in 1944 for the regions that originally had been under Italian rule. This gave the Jews living in the south of the country (who were also, for historical reasons, more assimilated with the Orthodox Christian Greek majority of the population) an opportunity to escape the persecution when it came.

Comrades.

Get strong and be brave.

A brilliant day, a day of great joy today, holiday of holidays, Passover great, day of redemption from a great calamity, today's day. We address heartfelt thanks to the King of Heavens for letting us live this day.

Gentlemen, the history of peoples is divided into large cycles, each turn of which closes one historical period and opens another new one.

The history of our people, so old and turbulent, is also divided into great circles, long periods that started and ended with great and dramatic events that disturbed its life and reshaped its historical progression.

13

The legend and tradition from the genealogy of our patriarch and founder Abraham to the exit from Egypt and the settlement in the land of Canaan is the first major turn in the history of the Jewish people.

The settlement in the Promised Land to the resettlement in Babylon—a cycle whose turn lasted a full thousand years—is the second great historical period of our people.

The return from Babylonian captivity to the destruction of the Second Temple, the "Beit Sheni," is the third historical period, and it lasted some six hundred years.

What follows is the great and adventurous turn of the cycle of Jewish history characterized by the uprooting of the Jewish people from the sacred territory of the land of Israel, the destruction and dismantling of the Jewish state, and the Diaspora of the Jewish people to the four corners of the globe.

The fourth historic period in the evolution of our people, which extended for over nearly 1,900 years, ends now. A fifth new period presents itself in front of us that may perhaps be called in our history "the period of our national Renaissance."

Influenced by the calamities that hit each one of us separately and all of us together, we are not yet in a position to appreciate the great change that these times have brought to our place and to our lives. When we recover from the wounds, when we have the power to reflect, then we will realize how different we have emerged from the recent fascist persecution.

An entire European state, with the most rigorous and disciplined internal organization, proclaimed against us ten years ago—without any provocation or cause on our part—the most cruel and relentless war of extermination. The real motives that moved the blond beast of the north to the most heinous and barbaric persecution of our race are most disgraceful and offend and stigmatize the entire civilized humanity. Never, since the recording of human history, in no time or place, has occurred what was forged and implemented in the past ten years of the twentieth century at the expense of an entire people from a large European state that was hitherto considered to be civilized.

All means, both intellectual and mechanical, that embellish modern life and that were intended to serve to make people's lives nicer and more bearable, all these intellectual and technical instruments and tools were leveraged by the blond beast of the north to conduct the premeditated and shamelessly acknowledged program of exterminating our people.

Even earlier in the course of our history, we encountered enemies and persecutors, but what will attract the attention of tomorrow's historian is that this despicable program has not been crafted and implemented by a single tyrant or by a single oligarchy. The entire German people as a state, as a nation, and as a social whole sought and pursued the evil extermination plan of our race.

The Germans could perhaps claim after their conclusive defeat, demanding to be believed, that World War II was provoked by Hitler's oligarchy without a mandate from or the approval of the German people. Those Germans who have the poor fortune to represent the defeated nation after the war may perhaps try to claim that the atrocious crimes committed by the German army in their occupied European countries burden only the Hitlerites and the Prussian militarists. No German, however, will have the audacity to want to confine the responsibility for the crimes against the Jewish people to a narrow circle of supporters of Hitler's party or of Prussian militarism, because Hitler's entire anti-Jewish extermination plan in its full extent and with all its detail was publicly proclaimed as the political program of Hitler's party, and the German people approved this program by means of free elections and by a large majority, bringing Hitler and his party to power.

The legal liability therefore of the entire German people for all the bad and horrible acts committed against us is obvious and self-evident. But equally obvious and indisputable is the political and moral responsibility of the German people for the felonies against us. Because throughout the ten-year period during which the entire civilized world was stunned by the news reports of anti-Jewish persecution, we did not see, either within Germany or outside, any worthwhile reaction by German officials against the implementation of Hitler's program of destruction and extermination.

We are therefore entitled, honorably and conscientiously, to express the condemning verdict against the entire German people for the development and the actual application of the program to destroy and eliminate our martyred nation.

15

As people peaceful and unaccustomed to confronting barbaric and medieval acts, we once liked to believe that those things being said and written against the Germans regarding their behavior against our racial brothers in other countries were exaggerated and excessive representations of the truth.

The German boot was destined, however, to step on and to infect even the sacred territory on the extreme point of the European continent that, with so much respect and so much reverence to its past greatness and its contemporary beauty, mankind names Hellas. We, too, were destined to know and to become eyewitnesses and scapegoats of the criminal fury of the hordes from the north, those hordes whose leaders with such sarcasm to the truth and with such arrogance claim to be supposedly the pinnacle of humanity.

The entire evil mechanism and refined system of Himmler and his rotten assault battalions were set into motion last year for the enslavement and the elimination of the eighty thousand Jewish residents of Greece. The start was made from the northern provinces, from the Macedonian metropolis, from Salonika, the *"Ir Vaem Beisrael,"* the mother city of Israel. There our poor brothers, psychologically unprepared, lacking direction, and misled by a corrupt and blameworthy communal leadership, were suddenly caught in the Himmlerian trap and kidnapped, almost in their totality, under conditions indescribable and horrific, as slaves in foreign and unknown countries, where every care and attention was taken for their fate to remain completely unknown to us.

The awful and abhorrent precedent set in the northern provinces—witnessed by God and by ourselves—and which last year shocked deeply the entire public sentiment of our country, this evil precedent contributed to the preparation of a disorganized yet effective passive resistance by the Israelites living in the southern provinces of Greece. Thanks to our disorganized but conscious self-defense, the rotten occupier was not able to complete his satanically planned and so patiently executed effort to enslave the country's remaining Jewish population.

To the Israelites of the district of Athens and to the person who gave the first gallant and courageous example of disobedience and resistance, the religious leader Elijah Barzilai, belong the honor that they preferred to be subjected to the agonizing test of a long passive resistance, a resistance that in each individual case is in itself an entire legend, a whole martyrdom, an entire history.

Each one of us can rightfully and proudly assert and proclaim that for twelve whole months, which seemed to us then like twelve whole years, with his life on the balance daily, conducted a truly herculean resistance fight against the organized Hitlerian state, from which fight we came out, by divine grace, victors.

This failure of our tyrants in the outskirts of the capital would have been even more resounding and humiliating for him if he had not obtained the cooperation and the assistance of two or three despicable agents who sadly bore Jewish names. The sad result of this treacherous and dishonest cooperation of these agents was that two thousand of our brothers here were arrested, beaten, stripped, tortured, and in certain known cases, even put to death. Divine nemesis and human justice will sooner or later fall heavily and mercilessly on the heads of these treacherous subhumans who soiled the Jewish name.

Ladies and gentlemen, it is useful on this historic moment for us to make a great realization precious for our future as individuals and as a whole: the realization that those of us who were blessed by God to survive the German persecution succeeded because at no time did we hesitate to expose our lives and to ignore our goods, our comforts, and our possessions. The Talmud, this inexhaustible treasure of Jewish wisdom, says somewhere that truly worthy of their freedom are those willing and able to seek it at all times. Let this be our first spiritual consolation and reward for those challenges that we suffered and for those bitter tears that we shed over the past terrible times. Let it also be an unforgettable example for our entire life and let it become a tradition and a testament for our children and our offspring.

It would be, however, unjust and inconsistent to say that, during the entire period of the persecution, we were only limited to passive resistance. Hundreds of young, our children and our brothers, especially some of those who were exempt of family obligations, resisted actively and bravely against the enemy in the Greek mountains, weapons in hands, in close and fraternal cooperation with the heroic rebel corps.

The corps and they have our full gratitude.

But much as our resoluteness may have been, gentlemen, and steady and strong our willingness to resist against the enemy, it would have been ineffective without another key and effective factor and contributor: the solidarity and assistance of the country's Greek population. Each of us is witness to the feelings of solidarity and acts of support demonstrated and provided by the Greek population as a whole toward us during the terrible days of persecution. If it is true that good friends are tested and proven in difficult circumstances, then it is undisputed that during these extremely difficult circumstances for us, the Greek population as a whole proved to be an excellent friend and worthy of our everlasting gratitude.

Dear brothers, at this moment of joy and self-reflection on our salvation from such major ills that only a few days ago were hanging like a Damoclean sword over our heads, we cannot forget our so many dead, our heroic lads who fought with such heroism in all battlefields against our country's fascist invaders and our people's enemies. We do not forget those of our brothers killed in vain, who in their effort to escape from the teeth of the rabid blond beast found an unjust and miserable death in the concentration camps of Haidari, Pavlos Melas, and elsewhere.

We also cannot stop focusing our thoughts constantly on those countless thousands of relatives and friends who were kidnapped so cruelly by our tyrants and who may be used now as laborers and slaves in who knows which inhospitable sites of the north and by who knows what new Pithom and Ramses for the construction of new, hideous pyramids to the glory of the sinister Hitlerian Moloch.

How much these brothers of ours in foreign lands resemble us and remind us of those of our ancestors who, two and a half thousand years ago, also had the misfortune to be kidnapped and to be uprooted from their beloved land of Israel and sent as slaves to Babylon and to decorate it with its hanging gardens. And our contemporary exiled brothers, like those of distant times, will not give in to the tyrants' invitations to sing in foreign lands the Songs of Zion but will repeat with courage and pride the unforgettable lyrics of Isaiah:

> By the rivers of Babylon,
> There we sat down and wept,
> When we remembered Zion.
> For there our captors demanded of us songs,
> And our tormentors mirth, saying,
> "Sing us one of the songs of Zion."
> How can we sing the Lord's song
> In a foreign land?
> *Im Eshkachech Yerusalaimtishkach yemini,*
> If I forget you, O Jerusalem,
> May my right hand forget her skill.
> May my tongue cling to the roof of my mouth
> If I do not remember you.[16]

Just as they returned one day and restored and extended the Temple of Solomon, the *Beit ha-Mikdash*, so in this current trial we hope in God that with them we will rebuild a new Jewish life, with new symbols and new live ideals in the old and historic country of our ancestors.

God never abandoned Israel.

Let us hope so. Perhaps better days will rise, and perhaps our current woes will be only forgotten dreams and memories.

Long live the immortal Jewry! Long live our Greece!

Postscript by Raphael Moissis

At age eleven, I remember listening ecstatically to this speech of my father's in the Old Synagogue of Athens, which was packed with surviving coreligionists who cried incessantly with emotion and grief the whole time.

---

16 Psalm 137

The opening word *"comrades"* is indicative of the times—this was before the Greek Civil War broke out a few weeks later in December of that year.

Asher Moissis delivering a speech at the Athens synagogue after the war. Standing to his left is the chief rabbi of Athens, Elias Barzilai.

Greeting to the Jews of Palestine

With emotion and with a heart clenched in pain, I address the Jews of Palestine to send them the first greeting from the few Jews in Greece who survived the decimation and destruction inflicted by the reprehensible German persecution.

When in April 1941, with the entry of the conqueror in Greece, we were cut off from the free world, seventy-five thousand Israelites lived here in Greece fraternally with the Greek people. Now there are only 8,300 of us left—in other words, only a tenth of how many there were. The other sixty thousand brothers were killed by asphyxiation by the Germans in the laboratories of death located in Auschwitz and Birkenau. If we few escaped death, we owe it to the Greek people in the mountains and the cities who helped us escape from the hands of the Huns.

As you know, the Jewish communities of Greece were some of the oldest and most renowned in the world and had been established two thousand years ago. For this reason, we the Jews in Greece are very much attached to this country and its people. Its joys are also our joys, and its sorrows are also our sorrows. In the Albanian war of 1940–41, nine thousand Jews of Greece fought in the Pindus Mountains. One thousand of them met death or were amputated for the freedom and honor of our foster homeland. Among these heroic victims, Colonel Mordechai Frizis, who fell in the first weeks of the war trying to defend an important strategic position on the Greek-Albanian border, deserves the first mention. But Jews from abroad also fought on Greek soil. Along with the British Expeditionary Force, which had arrived in Greece in April 1941, were one thousand Jews from Palestine. Two hundred of them fell in the battles of Olympus, while eight hundred others, determined to stay until the last minute in Greece, fell captive in the hands of the Germans in Kalamata.[17] Hence was renewed and sealed once again with blood the very old alliance and cooperation between Greeks and Jews that had started from the times of our King David who had formed his palace guard from handpicked Cretans.

This traditional cooperation will need to be relaunched now in peace projects thanks to the regeneration and restoration of the Jewish people in their ancestral homeland of Palestine.

The country of Greece is more Mediterranean than Balkan. So it will take its rightful seat in the new arrangement of Mediterranean issues. Furthermore, the national Jewish home of Palestine, which, as we all hope, will very quickly be declared an independent Jewish state, will become in the very near future a sizeable intellectual, political, and economic player for the eastern Mediterranean.

We Greeks and Jews are not only the oldest but also the smartest people in the world.[18] We must now apply these advantages. The Greek military and private citizens, who returned from Egypt and Palestine after the liberation of our country, have expressed to the Greek people their admiration for the amazing progress that Palestine has achieved in a few short years thanks to Jewish group colonization. This mutual introduction should be continued and extended. The establishment in Athens of a Greek-Palestinian trade chamber is now being considered. We, the few Jews who remain in Greece, will do everything we can to assist this effort. In Palestine a very old Greek community lives and prospers. And this should play a similar role.

Hence with this combined effort, with the natural leverage that the proximity of the two countries gives, and with the community of interests, we can anticipate a very close and very beneficial cooperation between the two peoples at the intellectual and economic level. Greeks and Jews, who in other times first cultivated and then transferred civilization from east to west, must now cooperate to transmit the new civilization from west to

---

17 The popular historical novel writer Leon Uris described this episode in his book *Angry Hills*.

18 Translator's note: And the most modest, too...

east. We believe that for this project they are the most appropriate and the most competent.

Putting into practice the cooperation between Greece and the Jews of Palestine that Asher Moissis had envisioned a few years earlier, Moissis (left) and David Ben-Gurion, then prime minister of Israel, visit the dam in Lake Marathon in December 1950.[19] Constructed in 1929, the lake and dam served as the main water supply for Athens until 1959.

---

19 This visit to Greece was actually David Ben-Gurion's first unofficial trip, two and a half years after he took over as prime minister of Israel. The purpose of his trip was to visit archeological sites and to search for old books. During his stay in Greece, he only had one official meeting, with the Greek prime minister, after the press became aware of his presence in the country.

First Gathering to Mourn the Victims of the Holocaust, Athens, March 1945

This speech was delivered in March 1945, only weeks after the liberation of Auschwitz, the largest death camp, on January 27, 1945. Other camps, such as Buchenwald, Dachau, and Mauthausen, were still under German control at this time. As survivors started to trickle out, the horrifying extent of the annihilation of European Jewry became apparent. Hitler was still alive, the battles were ongoing, and the allied armies steadily continued the occupation of Germany. The war in Europe was to end in early May.

Once again, Israel has a gathering for mourning, a gathering of tears and sorrow.

The bereavement is not for the loss of one of our dear ones, nor are the tears for the disappearance of one of our children.

The weeping is for many of our own; the ineffable sadness is for myriads of myriads of our brothers.

The lamentations of Jeremiah and the echo of the ramparts of Jerusalem would have been needed to express the feelings of pain and grief that fill our hearts for the terrifying loss of our people.

When our unexcelled psalmist, king, and prophet was found in a state of spiritual pain similar to the one that now grips our souls, he exclaimed,

> "Adonai, s'fatai tiftach u'fi yagid tehilatecha"
> "O Lord, open my lips,
> And my mouth shall show forth Your praise."[20]

The help of the Almighty is truly needed for human lips to dare speak about the immense, the inexpressible, the unbelievable disaster; about the

---

20 Psalm of David 51:15.

25

unhistorical and unimaginable tragedy that the Judaic race struck in these divinely cursed times.

Much as it is true that the long and eventful history of our race is associated with frequent and endless adventures, much as those adventures are so many and such as to allow a representative of modern Jewish thought, who is not even among the most pessimistic, to declare that you have to be blind not to see that the Jews are the people who were elected by fate for an endless suffering, nevertheless the human mind is left stunned and shocked by the unprecedented disaster that took place and may still be taking place in the heart of Europe, with the eternal and multitortured people of Israel as the victim.

Many of us believing in the natural law of progress and the perfection of man, carried away by the teachings of the progressive refinement of human instincts and the inevitable fraternization of the human race, had believed that religious and racial persecution, the pogroms, the manifestations of hatred and fanaticism, and the oppression of the weakest by the fittest belonged by now to history and constituted only a sad remembrance. The history of these last ten years came to refute the hopes of all those naive dreamers.

After the great human strife of the First World War, civilized mankind marched with a firm step along the path toward the attainment of the greatest human ideals. The League of Nations, general disarmament, united Europe, global security, and repudiation of war as an instrument of international law were slogans pervasive in the global public consciousness.

But while these great human ideals were cultivated and matured in the universal human consciousness, the enemy of international peace, the denier of human progress, the familiar international troublemaker lurked. The German nation, located in the center of the old civilized world and elevated, perhaps due to the presence within it of Semitic elements, to the pinnacle of modern engineering and technical progress, attempted for the second time in the twentieth century to undo the centuries-old, global governance based on international law and to impose on humanity a regime based on violence and destruction.

It is an error and an illusion to think that Nazism and its despicable theories are products of the unhealthy attitude and psycho synthesis of a single man, its staggering and hideous founder and leader. Just as wrong is the perception that Nazism constitutes an episodic and incidental phenomenon of the political life of the German people. A philosophical historical research of the political mental attitude of the Germans as a whole demonstrates that Hitlerism, with the variety of its manifestations—imperialism, anti-Semitism, the desire to overthrow international order, the repudiation of international law, the tendency to enslave small peoples, the enslavement of the power of the spirit to the violent state, the subjugation of the biblical ideal of universal love and brotherhood—all are an inalienable ideological property of the entire German people.

One still encounters people who wonder why Nazism proclaimed such a ruthless and devastating war against Judaism.

The explanation is simple: the Jews were everywhere and at all times elements of progress. Nazism is a reactive movement against the progressive spirit. Judaism taught, particularly by the mouth of a superhuman child, human love and respect for others. Hitlerism loudly proclaims hatred. The Jewish spirit proclaimed in various ways and even in the words of the founder of its child religion of Christianity, the Apostle Paul, that "there is no distinction between Jew and Greek, no distinction between slave and free man."[21] Hitlerism proclaims the superiority of the German over any other man. The Jewish Decalogue teaches respect for the goods of others. Hitlerism teaches and implements avidly the taking of goods if they do not belong to a German. Clearly, then, both complete the antithesis, and therefore their collision was inevitable and unavoidable. Never since the beginning of written human history could one find such a program of extermination, of such territorial scope, with such duration and such intensity, as the one applied by the Germans against the Jewish race in its entirety.

The annihilation of European Jewry by the frenzied National Socialism was not the result of an insurrection of the mob, one of those known to and investigated by the science of mob psychology.

---

21 Paul: Galatians 3:28.

This annihilation was not the result of the action of an electrified and angered crowd or of the storming of a besieged and resisting city. It resembles neither the Sicilian Vespers nor the raids of the vandals. It was an act designed satanically and plotted in all its macabre details by councils of governors and by military staffs.

Approximately six million of our brothers living in various European countries had the misfortune to find themselves under the rule of the German sword. Barbarian methods, centuries forgotten, were applied by specially organized and specifically trained German services. When, at the start of this great war, Poland first was occupied by the German motor swarms and two and a half million Jews were added to the other victims of Nazism, the world was suddenly informed that the region of Lublin had been identified by the German administration as a Jewish area within which the Jewish element established in the countries of central Europe under German sovereignty would be collected.

The unsuspecting mankind, not yet accustomed to the German methods—unprecedented in contemporary history—imagined that perhaps this was a false and hasty attempt to solve the Jewish question in Europe by applying the then-commonly proclaimed foolish theory of the separation of living spaces. For the first time, then, a surprised mankind, that which still breathed the air of freedom and was capable of being informed about international events, learned that entire Jewish populations were being uprooted forcibly from their homes and carried in convoys to the sinister Jewish space within horrible, hermetically closed railcars without food, without water, with no possibility to perform the most basic natural needs, and under the grip of Europe in total war.

All kinds of humiliation, every method of insult to human dignity, were set in motion intentionally and skillfully by the doctors of scientific extermination, Germans of the school of the notorious Rosenberg. So when the trains arrived at their destinations, the content comprised either of corpses or of scarcely alive human rags who had nothing in common with those decent and proud Jews, mostly scientists and intellectuals, before they were transformed into slaves.

There, in the inhospitable and icy plains of Silesia, death camps insurmountable in scientific perfection had been installed by the hideous executioners and slaughterers. The descriptions in Jewish publications in free countries of the methods applied in some of these death camps in Silesia, such as Majdanek and Birkenau, cause feelings of horror and revulsion. Hundreds of thousands of innocent men, women, and children found heinous and horrible death at these centers of mass extermination and slaughter only because they were of Jewish descent.

The hermetically sealed and tyrannical system of the German administration of the enslaved countries of Europe, where the drama of the slaughter of the Jewish race took place, has not yet allowed us to have a complete and detailed picture of the great and irreparable evil that was perpetrated. When, after a while, the last head of the Lernaean German Hydra is crushed and free communication is restored between the formerly enslaved European countries, then and only then will be revealed in all its aspects the heavy and dark veil that still covers the unimaginable drama of the Jewish people.

When the veil is uncovered in full, then all we survivors of the German persecution will compose the definitive account of the felonies of Nazism and will submit to the German people a bill for payment.

It is known that the principles of "an eye for an eye" and of "a tooth for a tooth" are attributed to the Jewish people as the law of retribution. We never considered this principle to be literal because it is incompatible with the spirit of forgiveness and humanism that inspires the entire Jewish morality.

Nevertheless, we do not hesitate to declare before God and men in this sacred hall that we will demand, for the punishment worth imposing on the Germans for their atonement of the felonies against our people, the removal not of an eye but eyes for an eye and not of a tooth but teeth for a tooth.

Following the declaration by the supreme religious authority of Jerusalem of an eight-day Jewish mourning everywhere in the world where living Jewish souls have survived, we arrive today to address a memorial and to kneel before the millions of innocent victims of German brutality. If it were possible for our spirit to communicate with the souls of these victims, we would send to them one message, a message of promise and consolation: the promise that we will avenge their unfair and tragic death and the consolation that

29

their death, at least this time, will not be for nothing and will have nothing in common with others of their race that occurred in past generations.

This time their own martyrdom and our own adventures contributed to awaken and to stimulate the human feeling of the Jewish people who survived the destruction, so that they shall be conscious of the demand for a new life, more dignified, collected, and national.

If we wish to address and to console sincerely the innocent souls of these millions of martyrs, we should not be satisfied with this revered memorial.

From the mass graves or from the mixed ash of the crematoriums, these victims demand that we follow with courage and self-denial the road that will lead us to a new life, more tolerant, more humane, more normal, a life different from that lived by those who were martyred; a life that will not give the ability or the opportunity to any new Hitler to confine it in sealed wagons and to transfer it to concentration camps and crematoriums; a life that, if ever it needs to be interrupted abruptly, can be interrupted with more dignity and more pride.

We are living through historic times. A great and tumultuous chapter in the history of the Jewish people closes permanently with the storm that sank and eliminated the bulk of our brothers in Europe while allowing the few of us to swim.

If this chapter of Jewish history has closed, this does not mean that the history of the Jewish people has ceased or that the development of Jewish life has been interrupted. We are an old people, and our strength and our endurance has been tested repeatedly in the course of the centuries.

We proved that we are capable of surviving our persecutors, whether they are called Ashur or Vespasian or Torquemadas or Hitler. How many times was it not repeated with a sense of pain but also with triumph from our blood-dripping but also unyielding lips the verse of our great bard?

"They break in pieces thy people, O Lord.[22]
They are brought down and fallen:
But we are risen, and stand upright"[23]

The German persecution left us missing a large portion of our people. It left us uprooted from our homes, deprived of our financial assets. The few of us, however, who survived both far from our homes and deprived of our property are sufficient and capable both to punish our pursuers and to guarantee the resurrection of our race.

We hope always that, except for us who were fortunate to regain the coveted freedom, many others of our brothers, numerous perhaps, still exiles and slaves today, will survive and increase our ranks. When the blessed day of their liberation and their return comes, then we will undertake with them the regrouping and the restoration of our house, taking care that the ground on which we build is stable and its foundations are firm so as to withstand any new shocks.

And then we will neither organize memorials nor recite Jeremiah, but we will sing in chorus the first pleasant and optimistic musical psalm:

"When the Lord bringeth back our people from captivity
Jacob shall rejoice
And Israel shall be glad."[24]

---

22 Psalm 94:5.

23 Psalm 20:8.

24 Psalm 14:7.

PANEGYRIC FOR THE END OF WORLD WAR II

Asher Moissis delivered this speech in Athens on Sunday, May 20, 1945, to celebrate the capitulation of Germany and the end of World War II in Europe. The war of the Allies in the Pacific against Japan, which would continue until August of that year, was very distant in the hearts and minds of the speaker and his audience.

The Central Council of the Jewish Communities of Greece, the Jewish Community of Athens, and the Zionist Federation are pleased that by extraordinary fortune their surviving members meet at this holy place desecrated by the occupier and resanctified to praise the Lord on the occasion of the victorious end of the war. And we are also pleased that the ceremony was dignified and honored by the presence of members of the government, political leaders, members of the diplomatic corps, and representatives of the city of Athens and of Greek public opinion.

This celebration of victory gives to us Israelites especially, for the first time after long years of persecution and lamentations, the opportunity to set aside our heavy grief and to forget the pain that rips our deeply wounded hearts.

The celebration of this victory and of the end of the bloodshed cannot, unfortunately, be followed for us Jews by enthusiastic events and by an outpouring of joy and exultation because our pain still drowns the joy and our suffering still extinguishes the enthusiasm.

The call of victory is for us a simple historic date, a date that gives us the opportunity to pause mentally, to reflect, to take account of our sacrifices—an account tragically gruesome—to remember those who fell while fighting and those lost while persecuted, to regroup and to give the signal for a new collective start.

The history of nations is divided into major periods in their evolution and development, into large historical cycles that begin and end under the influence of decisive and fateful events and phenomena. No nation on Earth has escaped the influence of these rotations caused by fateful and unexplored natural and sociological causes.

The Jewish nation also has its historic fate. Appearing at the forefront of human history, alongside the Greek nation, with the first steps of human civilization, it experienced all the twists and turns that the mystery of life conceals, from the highest peaks that brightened it to the inglorious declines that darkened and humiliated it.

During this course through the centuries, Jewish thought succeeded at some point in time to rise up to the sky and to meet divinity. This was achieved while other nations, unknown still to history and ungrouped, lived barbarous and cannibal-like lives at the northern edge of continental Europe. When these cannibals, thanks to their brush with the advanced civilization of the Mediterranean, reached a vague cultivation of their thought, the only thing to which they aspired was the worship of the Valkyries and the Nibelungen and the coarse apotheosis of a blind hero and his wild instincts.

With the exception of the Greek nation, no other people on Earth have had such a long and eventful history as ours. Originating four thousand years ago from the springs of the Euphrates, with a founding father who was later recognized as the originator of the finest part of humanity, it established itself in that small coastal strip of the eastern Mediterranean that became its homeland and subsequently the fatherland of all of humanity that shares our ideals.

We enjoyed free national life in this delightful place twenty-four centuries, during which we developed our racial ability and virtue, created a prototype civilization that grounds human life in love, justice, and humanism. Immersed almost exclusively in the cultivation of these spiritual ideals of domestic life, we neglected to care for the maintenance and safeguarding of our free national entity. Thus, when Roman catapults struck in their turn the walls of our national and spiritual center, Jerusalem was razed and transformed into Aelia Capitolina; our assembled national life gave way to the Diaspora, and since then we are planets at the ends of the Earth bringing with us everywhere the only portable good of the Palestinian land not subject to wear and tear, our Bible.

To preserve our life during this long and turbulent period of dispersal, we paid a price incomparably higher than the price borne by other peoples for their national existence and independence.

We were unfortunately bound to endure in these recent terrible times the heaviest price, the most terrifying strike and most destructive devastation known in the entire two-thousand-year history of our Diaspora.

Mankind had just begun to feel itself safe and to entrust its fate in the progress and conquests of the spirit. High-minded principles, sermons of eternal peace, and definitive fraternization of people were proclaimed widely and extensively. People had believed that the fullness of time, which our prophets had first presaged and the unexcelled Nazorean later evangelized, had finally arrived.

And to be true, after so much sacrifice and such progress in all aspects of life, mankind had the right to hope and to believe that a future free from the dark adventures of the past was in store for it. The organization of the international existence of countries had also progressed in such a way that there was a hope that international relations would be based on the sense of mutual respect and would be regulated by an appropriate body of world recognition and world prestige.

A nasty fate, however, intervened and suspended and interrupted this course of virtue. The forces of evil contemplated with envy the progressing humanity and, as if they had not been satiated by the blood that for so many centuries they had absorbed, falling with all their ferocity upon the unsuspecting humanity, reinitiated the task of devastation and destruction. These forces of evil originated from and were once again nursed and matured in the same territory and in the midst of the same nation through which they had appeared and had developed and had committed their felonies just a few years before, in the very same heart of Europe that was praised for its culture and progress.

These forces of devastation that stained the twentieth century, disrupted world order, and doubted and denied the centuries' accepted principles of virtue, human altruism, and justice, appeared and matured and operated again through the German nation.

Never, in no time in history and in no place inhabited by men, did the primitive instincts of savagery and of barbarism find a more despicable incarnation and a more appalling manifestation than the ones these instincts found in the pronouncements and teachings of hate contained in the theories of Hitlerism.

"Our animals are useless henceforth," wrote Hitler in his book *Mein Kampf*, "because instead of animals we have the inferior races." What contempt and what sarcasm for the superior divine nature of mankind!

To serve and justify the new selfish German ideal, the theory of separation of the races was invented. As would be expected, the German nation was placed at the highest rank of racial nobility; and because it was indispensable to serve hatred and envy, the Jewish race was placed on the lowest rung of the racial hierarchy.

Those miserable ones! They derided the eagle that once had flown so high as to reach the heavens and to meet the deity, because, after they cut its wings, it is now unable to fly high.

Antiquity also had chosen peoples. We used to take pleasure in declaring ourselves "the Lord's chosen people." Our distinctiveness, however, we associated neither with the nobleness of our flesh nor with the purity of the blood in our veins but with the distinctiveness and nobleness of our spirit, which dominates matter, with the superiority of our civilization, and with the supremacy of our laws and our institutions. "One law and one rule shall be for you and for the stranger who sojourns with you," said the Lord.[25]

The ancient Greeks also boasted with justifiable pride that "all non-Greeks are barbarians" but added with emphasis that "whoever speaks the Greek language is a Hellene." This signified that those who would be considered and recognized as Greek did not necessarily and not only include those who drew their descent directly from Deucalion and from Xuthus but every person privy to the mysteries of the wonderful Greek thinking, regardless of his or her origin, descent, and blood.

The Germans did not limit themselves of course to a peaceful declaration of their supremacy but resolved to levy its recognition by the sword

---

25 Book of Numbers 15:16.

upon other nations they sought to subjugate. And for the execution of this arrogant and rash claim, they unleashed the fiercest and most brutal of wars that recent human generations have known, a war that was more like an attack of piratical and predatory hordes against an unsuspecting camp of resting humans than a contest between nations fighting to defend their national claims.

In this war, original in its causes and in its declaration and in its means and instruments of conduct and in its goals and purposes, fate wished to see engaged the country, small in its extent but large in its history and its name, in which for centuries we, too, had been established and inhabited as its equal children, our Greek homeland.

One could say that Greece's participation in a war conducted for the defense of those principles and goals that embody the Hellenic ideal was fated and inevitable.

The Greeks courageously proved from the first days of the extension of the war to their borders that they were inspired by the same feelings that guided their ancestors in classical times when they fought for the preservation of Greek civilization from the raids of the precursors of today's barbarians and deniers of the ideas of freedom and human dignity.

We are proud that in the gloriously crowned struggle of the Greek youth in the Albanian mountains and in the Macedonian ridges, the Israelite citizens of the Greek homeland along with numerous children of the resurrected in the Palestinian national Jewish home, who rushed to join the ranks of the British Expeditionary Force to support the Greek struggle, also participated and displayed no lesser a sense of patriotism and self-sacrifice. The name and the war action of the Greek-Jewish colonel Frizis, who was one of the first to fall in the legendary Pindus Mountains, will always come first in our memory and will guide us to the fulfillment of our duties to our foster homeland.

In this titanic struggle, in which all those values that adorn the life of free people were at stake, the greatest sacrifices were indisputably made by the Jewish nation.

All the hatred, all the power, all the weight, and all the infernal means available to the German war machine were set in operation and in use with great care and evilness for the success of one of the priority projects of Germanism, namely the destruction and annihilation of the Jewish race.

The Greek people, who experienced for three and a half years the burden of the German yoke, were witness to the brutality and the atrocities set in motion in our country as well by the grim conqueror for the execution of the project of proscription and extermination of the Jewish element that lived for so many centuries in Greece. Unknown until just recently remained only one aspect of the whole tragedy, an aspect that is just beginning to be revealed and displays the image of the most horrendous drama that unfolded upon the world for as long as human history has been recorded.

The veil now being uncovered reveals that the systematic persecution and group deportation of Jews from all countries of occupied Europe, which unfortunately included sixty thousand Greek citizens of our race, aimed neither at their enslavement nor at other goals related to military security or servicing other military objectives but targeted the very premeditated killing of the displaced, conducted with such terrifying and dreadful and inhuman methods that, when described, convulse the soul and the body of the audience until they shudder and become literally incredulous.

Infants, children, elderly, disabled, men and women, without distinction, without cause, and without provocation, after being subjected to horrific humiliation and brutality, were conducted to the scientific laboratories of death that the German culture had deliberately devised and installed and were killed in thousands and myriads.

Over four million such innocent Jewish human beings found tragic death in these horrible workshops of death of Silesia. The human mind pauses before such a treatment of man by man, and the humane feeling blushes with shame for its unprecedented decline.

But the eye of justice exists that sees all.[26] The German monster, after committing its felonies and causing such devastation and spreading so many tears, was finally struck at its core by the punishing Allied forces of the

---

26 In Greek: "ἔστι δίκης Ὀφθαλμός ὅς τά πάνθ' ὁρᾷ", a quote attributed to the ancient Greek dramatist Menander.

United Nations and now expires before the eyes of the amazed and fully outraged humanity.

If *justice* in this world is not an empty and meaningless word, then it is essential that these unheard-of crimes be punished and atoned for. We Jews, who suffered in this circumstance more than anyone else the injustice, know and feel more than anyone else how desirable and necessary justice is.

All of Germany as a national and spiritual whole is responsible toward us and toward humanity, and as such it must be punished. If this does not happen, or if it does not happen to the appropriate degree, this omission will constitute the greatest slap to the international moral order.

And then we will rightly be able to repeat for the account of and to the face of humanity the indicative phrase of Shakespeare: "I crave the law."[27]

Until this punishment is imposed, every Jewish mouth, every Jewish voice, will declare and shout from every official and informal podium that standard incantation of the Roman senator: "Censeo Germaniam Delendam Esse."[28]

We would nonetheless be unsophisticated and would prove to be ignorant of the long experience of our vast national life if our aspirations and our demands centered only on the purification of the past. The past in its own right is only worthy of interest if it is to serve the future. History is not written and read only to satisfy people's curiosity but also to provide lessons for the future.

We are therefore obliged, on this historic moment, when we transition from the state of war to the order of peace, to take the pulse carefully of our organism and to diagnose its weak signs.

This probing and self-examination, undertaken with courage and objectivity, compel us to arrive at certain conclusions.

Nazism was a global scourge, a microbe that spread across the entire earthly atmosphere. This microbe struck many state and national organizations. All those affected were sickened by its presence. Each offended body,

---

27 William Shakespeare, *The Merchant of Venice*, IV, 1, 214 (spoken by Shylock the Jew when he is encouraged by Portia to be merciful).

28 The reference here is to the Roman statesman Cato the Elder, who routinely ended his speeches with the phrase "Carthage must be destroyed" (Carthage was indeed fully destroyed after the Third Punic War).

however, reacted in different ways and to different degrees, and the disease that had been introduced had several developments and complications.

And just as Pasteur said, the impact of the microbe depends, usually in a decisive way, on the endurance and the general constitution of the object.

Nazism prevailed temporarily throughout the European continent. It attempted to implement its rogue plans wherever it dominated, from the northernmost Norway to our southernmost country. All these conquered countries and these enslaved people contracted the Hitleric epidemic and suffered and were weakened. Of all the organisms afflicted, however, the Jewish organism was the one that was affected the most, became most gravely ill, and weakened most terribly. This forces us in a logical reasoning to admit and to recognize that Jewry, when examined as a whole, suffers from a hazardous organic weakness.

As individuals, the Jews are perhaps one of the strongest nations of the world; as a people, as a whole, however, they are the weakest. This simultaneous power and weakness constitutes the main cause for the Jewish tragedy across the centuries. As long as the problem of the Jewish people, as an organic whole, does not find its just and historic solution, then the problem of the Jew as an individual will also remain fatefully and eternally unsolved.

The huge sacrifices of the Jewish people from all countries, both on the battlefront and in the rear, during the universal conflict that just concluded, added new powerful titles that allow us to hope that, in the next Peace Conference, a definite solution will be given to the age-old Jewish problem, a solution in accordance with the aspirations of the Jewish people and the pronouncements of the Allied states for the freedom and self-determination of nationalities but also in the common good of all humanity.

These titles of sacrifice are compounded by the great advances that were achieved in recent years by the Jewish people in the Palestinian national home, advances that cause global admiration and prove that the Jewish people are perfectly mature and worthy of occupying a position of equality in the family of nations.

If it is fateful that national causes are solved and national aspirations are vindicated with sacrifices in blood, then these sacrifices we suffered and this price of liberty we paid at an extremely high cost in the last war.

We enter the period of peace with the conviction and hope that our fates as individuals and as a national whole will be subjects of concern for the governments and the international organizations of peace. Our relentless persecution by the conqueror, the annihilation of most of our brothers, the looting of our goods, and the removal from our homes also brought about restoration problems that are agonizing for us. The Greek government, continuing its tradition and conforming to the liberal spirit of the Greek people with friendly and unbiased policy toward the Jewish element, follows and manages our problems with understanding and sympathy.

We do not overlook the difficulties faced by the government to restore a normal social life to the country, difficulties that understandably delay the addressing and resolution of the problems that concern us. The restitution of confiscated property to the surviving Israelites and the establishment of a special agency for the collection and diligent administration of abandoned Jewish property is undoubtedly one of the burning issues that need to be addressed urgently. Resolution of these issues is being monitored by the surviving Jewish population of the country with obvious impatience, which is justified by the dire financial position in which it found itself following the relentless German persecution.

Concluding my speech, I feel obligated to express on behalf of all Jews our ardent thanks to His Beatitude the Viceroy, to the honorable members of government, to the representatives of the Allied states, to the political leaders, to the mayor of Athens, and to all other guests for the pleasure of accepting our invitation to honor today's ceremony with their presence.

Sunday, May 20, 1945

First Annual Memorial for the Holocaust Victims, 1946[29]

One more mournful celebration will be added for eternity to the Jewish holiday calendar that reflects so faithfully and externalizes so vividly the internal life of our people; another fast; another mourning: the eternal memorial, the great yeshiva, for our innumerable dead fathers, sons, and brothers who were martyred on the altar of the German deity of hatred.

Until a unique and single day for this pan-Judaic contemplation is set by a worldwide Jewish synod, the memorial service will be conducted in each country on a day that is locally closer to the chronology of the great drama.

With a circular to all communities, the Central Jewish Council appointed this day for us to commemorate our sixty thousand martyrs. All of the country's communities established today for this general mourning.

We gather therefore in this sacred place, which also happens to be the place from where two years ago many of our brothers departed for their fateful trip.

Ever since, two thousand years ago, we lost our national independence and began the Diaspora of our people, we have received continual blows and faced endless persecution and destruction. The history of the Jewish people after the destruction of the Second Temple resembles a history of racial and religious persecution.

In ancient times we were one of the greatest nations in the world. If the Diaspora had not ensued and conditions of normal national life existed for our people, we would today be one of the more numerous and powerful nations on earth. We resemble a tree with strong roots and a sturdy trunk, but because it is planted in foreign soil, its branches are cut off every once in a while on the pretext that they prevent the comfortable development and breathing of the surrounding foliage.

---

29 Only a fragment of this speech, published here, survives.

People are always very creative when it comes to discovering pretexts and triggers to rid themselves of the presence of other fellow men. Especially when these are Jews, the imagination is unrivaled.

The Jews poison the wells. Death to the Jews.

The Jews make human sacrifices to use Christian blood for Passover. Fire and axe to the Jews.

They are usurers; they raise prices and collect the gold; they are social revolutionaries, are [two illegible words] of the very homeland; they belong to a lower race.

For all these and for each one of them individually, Jews must be destroyed.

With such ridiculous pretexts, with such foolish slogans, a full six million Jews were sent to their graves—but woe even beyond the graves because there are no graves for them; more than one-third of the Jewish race, with no accusation, no sentence, only because they were Jews.

This crime is unprecedented in the history of humanity. It is unprecedented in the Jewish history of endless persecution and suffering, neither because of the frighteningly large number of victims nor for the unprecedented temporal and spatial extent but because it was inspired, planned, and executed not by hordes of a fanatic mob but by a formal and responsible government. And it was inspired and designed and executed not in a momentary emotional impulse but in a state of mental sobriety for those who conceived and decided and executed it.

The minutes of the international war criminals trial in Nürnberg reveal that the decision for the mass extermination of Jewish residents in the German-occupied countries of Europe had been made in the month of November of the year 1942 with every solemnity, probably at a cabinet meeting of the German government. Here exactly lies the great gravity and the unprecedented nature of the sinister and heinous crime. A government, which included among its members scientists, and at the peak of the twentieth century and in the heart of Europe, a government elected by a proper vote by an entire people, studied, designed, and set into motion a decision that even the dirtiest savages of the most vulgar caverns would hesitate to plan and conceive. If we believe in the saying that each people is worthy of its government, then we should believe that the German people deserved this government of criminal officials.

Executor of this horrific murderous plan for the Jews in our country was the infamous Captain Dieter Wisliceny. As he most cynically disclosed during the trial of Nürnberg, where, surprisingly, he was examined as a witness on January 3, 1946, he was sent to Salonika in January of 1943 by order of one of the heads of the gestapo, Eichmann.[30] There, with a most satanic plan, he collected fifty thousand of our unsuspecting and defenseless brethren, whom, stacked in the familiar railcars of death, he transferred to the memorably horrific Auschwitz, where they were killed most scientifically by the thousands. The same German executioner, in September of the same year, 1943, a few days after the assumption of the administration of all of Greece by the Germans, came to Athens and attempted to devise the same insidious extermination plan; he was unsuccessful in implementing it immediately and entirely. The signal of defiance and resistance was given in a timely manner, and so the executioner was forced to defer the enactment of his plan by a full six months. During this period, several hundreds of our brothers, either lured by the inducement of paid agents of the enemy who carry, unfortunately, Jewish names or forced for financial reasons to comply with the orders of the enemy, were caught in the trap set within this sacred hall and were led from here to the site of martyrdom.

Of the 7,500,000 Jews who lived in the occupied countries of Europe, only 1,200,000 survived. Eighty-seven percent of the total Jewish population was lost in this way; only 13 percent survived. From Greece, where 75,000 Jews lived, only 10,000 survived, and nearly everyone else perished. We, too, thus lost 87 percent in our country, and only 13 percent remained alive. Of our country's twenty-four Jewish communities, fourteen lost more than 90 percent of their members and were disbanded, another four lost more than 50 percent, and all others, outside of Athens, lost more than 25 percent of their population.

---

30 At the time of this speech, Adolf Eichmann was in hiding. He eventually made his way to Argentina, where he hid until his abduction by an Israeli commando unit in 1961. He was tried in Jerusalem, convicted, and hanged in 1962. His ashes were then dispersed in the Mediterranean, outside Israel's territorial waters.

These grim statistics give a rough idea of the great tragedy that struck the Jewry of Europe in general and of our country in particular. They simultaneously give an image of the moral and material ruin caused elsewhere and in our country by the German storm. The tasks of restoring these ruins and rebuilding Jewish life are as difficult as was terrible the shock that caused the collapse.

For this restoration and rebuilding, certain conditions are required:

1. The assistance and cooperation of major Jewish care organizations abroad;
2. The governmental [The manuscript is interrupted here.]

MAX MERTEN TRIAL — FEBRUARY 1959

The name of Nazi officer Max Merten became associated in Greece not only with the extermination of the Jews of Salonika but also with the country's political circumstances in the late fifties. Merten came to Greece for unknown reasons in 1958 and was sentenced by the Special Military Court of Athens in February 1959 to a "combined imprisonment" of twenty-five years. A few months later, according to the rulings of a special law approved by the Greek Parliament, he was extradited to West Germany to serve his sentence there. In 1960 he was released.

Asher Moissis was one of the top, if not the leading, witness at the trial of Max Merten. His testimony at the Military Court took place on February 16, 1959, lasted five whole hours, and was characterized by the royal commissioner as "clear and impartial," while the next day's press wrote that "there could not have been a more appropriate witness."

He himself in his March 6 letter to Joseph Nehama, who had hastened to congratulate him on his testimony, writes, "My testimony was an epitaph to the graveless memorials of our own forty-five thousand, a sort of kaddish for all those known and unknown individuals who were sacrificed unfairly." In the same letter, he states that "My testimony was not recorded, and no newspaper published it exactly." He refers, however, to the newspaper Ethnos as most accurately portraying the content of his testimony.

The following texts originate from
 a. A typewritten text from the archives of Asher Moissis that is, in all likelihood, his testimony to the investigator prior to the trial.
 b. Newspaper clippings from February 17. All these clippings are found in the same archive.

SWORN TESTIMONY TO THE INVESTIGATOR

Up until March 3, 1941, I was a lawyer in Salonika. I also served in 1933 and thereafter as president of the local Jewish Community and of other Jewish organizations and foundations there. Predicting my certain persecution by the German authorities if they occupied Salonika, I departed thence as soon as I sensed the unfortunate for the country imminent developments; I fled to Athens, where, discovered by the occupation authorities, I was pursued. I was one of the few who were rescued miraculously.

After the liberation of Greece, I was entrusted by the Greek government with the reorganization of the Jewish communities and the establishment of the Central Jewish Council and the Relief and Rehabilitation Agency of the Jews of Greece (OPAIE), the leadership of which I left in 1949 and 1950, having been appointed first consul and later the diplomatic representative of the State of Israel to Greece, a position I held up to 1954.

As a result of these associations, I observed with special interest the entire drama of the persecution of the Jewish element of Greece and in particular that of Salonika by the German occupation authorities, played a leading role in the defense and rescue of a portion of the population, and collected numerous items to write and publish for historical purposes.

I drew the data and information concerning the activities of the accused Max Merten from my personal interventions with the Greek government in Athens in 1942 and 1943 for the rescue of my persecuted coreligionists; and by the authentic information that was transmitted to me by my longtime partner and colleague, the late Yomtov Yakoel, after he escaped to Athens from Salonika in July 1943. Until his escape to Athens, he was the mastermind of the Jewish Committee on Social Welfare, which, under this camouflaged name, undertook the work of defending from the German persecution of the Jewish element of Salonika.

My partner hid first with me in Kifissia under the false name of Aristotelis Georgiades and then in Neo Heraklion in Attica. There he began to write his memoirs on the persecution of the Jewish element of Salonika from the entry of the German army in the Macedonian capital. He was able to include with all detail, objectivity, and authenticity the events up to the eve of his deportation, when his hideout was betrayed by heinous, collaborationist traitors, and he was arrested by the Germans, at five in the afternoon on Wednesday, December 22, 1943. He was then displaced via the camp in

Haidari to Birkenau in Poland, where he and his family were killed in horrendous circumstances.

These manuscripts—memoirs, having been rescued, were handed to me on the very day of his arrest (December 22, 1943) and are now in my possession. They were published in installments in the Athens newspaper *Evraiki Estia*, and I submit photocopies of the pages relating to the actions of the accused.

In summary, based on the evidence that either fell to my own awareness or was transmitted to me by others; and specifically:

1. by the then archbishop of Athens Damaskinos;
2. the then prime minister Logothetopoulos;
3. the then metropolitan of Thessaloniki Gennadios;
4. the personal narratives of Yomtov Yakoel and other Salonikans;
5. but especially from the memoirs I hold of Yomtov Yakoel, whose authenticity and sincerity and accuracy I consider beyond doubt and dispute;

the following facts regarding the actions of the accused are established:

1. This man, because of the widespread power vested upon him by the German military administration of Salonika, became a true tyrant and satrap of the city and is responsible for very many executions (without trial) of Greek citizens, Christians and Jews, for imprisonments, persecutions, for the looting of property and even for blackmail.
2. This man should be considered as the main person responsible for the enlistment in July 1942 of eighteen-to-forty-five-year-old males into forced labor, which was ordered by the German military administration of Salonika-Aegean, during which hundreds of them died from hardship, disease, and executions on the spot.
3. This man is the main instigator and perpetrator of the agreement signed in Salonika on October 17, 1942, in the basement of the Jewish Charity Foundation soup kitchen Matanoth Laevioneim on Mizrachi Street, between the Jewish community of Salonika and the accused,

who personally signed the relevant protocol on the redemption of the Jews' forced labor, against three and a half billion drachmas (of which two billion in cash and one and a half based on the price of the land of the cemetery). The role played by the accused in this case is characteristic, acting with complete initiative, going thrice in person to the Matanoth Foundation, accepting or rejecting proposals, and finally signing the relevant protocol, as established from Yomtov Yakoel's detailed account.

4. The very accused should be considered a co-perpetrator or necessary accomplice of the events that followed the redemption of the forced labor, namely the predatory measures of the displacement and killing in Auschwitz-Birkenau of the approximately forty-five thousand Jews of Salonika; his actual liability as co-perpetrator or necessary accomplice becomes self-evident from the following events:

   a. The German officers Wisliceny and Bruner, who arrived from Germany to implement the measures of displacement and killing, namely the "final solution," according to the documents revealed at the Nürnberg trial, would not have had the material strength to disrupt and destroy an entire population of forty-five thousand people without the support and cooperation of the German occupying army in Salonika, which took orders from the military administration and which, again, as far as issues not purely military were concerned, was represented by the accused.

   b. Because Yakoel explicitly narrates in his memoirs that upon the arrival of the executioners Wisliceny and Bruner in Salonika the Jewish Community received a document from the German military administration dated February 6, 1943, ordering that thereinafter the community was subject to the direct orders of these executioners and forcing the community to take measures aimed at facilitating the displacements.

   c. Because during the signature of the redemption protocol, the accused Merten had given his word that, after this buyout, no other persecution measure would be applied against the Jewish element, and this promise, having been disclosed, led the Jewish population to believe that it was hereafter safe and hence it did not seek to escape the danger. The late Yakoel in the summary of the last chapter of his memoirs, which he did not have the time to finish, writes the following: "rumors about a displacement and reassurance of the public opinion by Dr. Merten."

Thus, the accused Merten, by means of fraud and persuasion, misled the unfortunate Israelites to remain in their places. Had he been uninvolved in this heavy responsibility, he should have resigned his position. Not only did he not do so, but on the contrary, it has been certified that he appeared at the train station during the departure of the first "death trains" from Salonika to Auschwitz.

The German plan of the "final solution" was so devilish that I do not exclude that this promise was delivered by the accused to the representatives of the Israelites of Salonika to tranquilize them and make them easier victims for the implementation of their sinister plans.

I remember in this connection what a Jewish mother had told me in 1944, while the persecution in Athens was under way. During her appearance with her young child at the synagogue for the weekly "attendance," the German SS officer present would approach and caress the young Jewish children; the poor woman expressed to me the conviction that "it was not possible to expect something evil from people who show such delicate feelings toward young children."

The very same German executioner, however, on the predetermined date of March 24, 1944, entrapped eight hundred Jews of Athens who had arrived to give their "attendance" at the synagogue and sent them to the gas chambers of Auschwitz, along with the children that he so affectionately pampered and with the mother who had believed in his evil cajolery.

COMPILATION OF NEWSPAPER CLIPPINGS – FEBRUARY 17, 1959

The most substantial witness yesterday was Mr. Asher Moissis, consul of Israel in Greece from 1950 to 1954, a lawyer, historical author, and one of the leading figures of the Jews in Greece. His testimony, which covered the

entire morning session of the military court, was the most scathing accusation against Merten up to now. The discussion between the court judges and
the witness, the defense, and the accused was held with absolute silence in the
room. The witness referred to the entire activity of the accused by means of
audited data and enlightened the court on many hitherto unknown aspects
of the occupation period.

WITNESS: From Athens, where I moved due to the events of the occupation, I followed the life and fate of my coreligionists in Salonika. On the
subject, I had a continuous and detailed cooperation on all matters with the
legal adviser of the Jewish community of Salonika, Attorney Yakoel, who was
executed by the Germans.

It was our ill fate that brought Merten to Salonika. Immediately after
his arrival, the great persecution of the Jews began. In his manuscript, which
was delivered to me when he was arrested so that I could preserve it, Yakoel
reports that all measures against the Jews were by order of Merten. He had
said then that before the war he had been a prosecutor in Germany and a
reserve officer in Salonika. After the liberation, I discovered through multiple
sources that, before the occupation, Merten was a simple practicing lawyer
in Berlin. This, however, did not prevent him from applying tortures worse
even than those of medieval times.

PRESIDENT: What do you know, Mr. Witness, about the buyout of the
forced labor and the rest of the accusations?

WITNESS: Miller, the Greek project developer, had proposed to Yakoel
the redemption of the forced labor of the Jews after visiting them at the
projects in the region of Komotini, where the Jews worked ill with fever and
housed in stables...This is the beginning.

PRESIDENT: Who was this Miller? Was he prosecuted?

WITNESS: He was a collaborator with the Germans. I do not know
whether he was prosecuted. In any case, a few days later, Merten, the
almighty general of Salonika, enters into negotiation with the stake-
holders in the basement of the house of a Jew. Initially he asked for 3.5
billion drachmas, and he eventually agreed to close the agreement for
twenty thousand pounds plus the materials of the cemetery, the entire
cemetery.

The Jews told him that the holy law prohibits the exhumation of the dead. The Germans then destroyed it and sold the gravestones and the bricks.

I submit to the court a telegram by the grand rabbi of Salonika to the Jews in Athens requesting that they assist in the collection of the aforementioned amount.

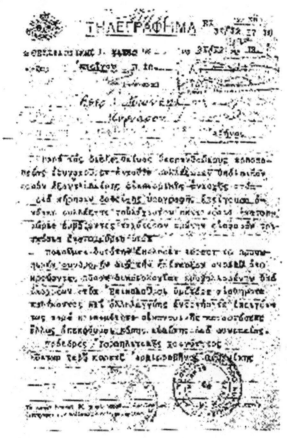

A telegram by the grand rabbi of Salonika to the Jews in Athens requesting that they assist in the collection of funds demanded by Max Merten.[31]

---

31 The telegram reads as follows:
Telegram

The installments were paid to Merten correctly. Based on what Yakoel, Amarilio (who lives in Athens), and Arouch had told me, the money was collected in the National Bank from which they obtained a check that Merten did not agree to receive because he wanted cash. Consequently, they cashed the check and handed over the cash in his office at the Koniordos Mansion.

ROYAL COUNCILLOR: Why did he not want a check?

WITNESS: I have the same question, Mr. Councillor. How did this terrible military administrator go in secret with Meissner to close the deal?

ROYAL COUNCILLOR: Why, defendant, did you not invite the official representatives of the Jews to your office and negotiate there? Why did you prefer the night and the basements of houses instead of the day's sun?

MERTEN (standing to attention, reddened as always and with a booming voice): There was a war, Mr. Councillor. There were orders from the Ministry of Security that we should not only not help the Jews but also that we should persecute them. I started the negotiations, violating this prohibition for the sake of the weak Jews who were dying in the streets. Had I received even one representative in my office, I would have been executed on the spot.

ROYAL COUNCILLOR: How did you act? Did you have related orders to request the 2.5 billion drachma amount, or were you operating without your superiors' knowledge and by your own initiative?

From: Salonika, No. 16152, time 13
Date: 31/12/42
URGENT
To: Asher Moissis, 3 Kornarou St., Athens
Despite the superhuman efforts made, we are unable at this point to collect the balance of the amount, having exhausted our financial capacity—stop. To adhere to the signature that was given, there is an urgent need for you to collect at least five hundred million and deposit as soon as possible a first infusion of three hundred million—stop. I make this ultimate request to you to provide your personal assistance to achieve this goal, countering any excuse made by those obligated—stop. I appeal to your sense of duty and allegiance to act urgently despite the critical financial situation; otherwise, I take no responsibility for the consequences.
The President of the Jewish Community
Dr. Sewy Koretz, Chief Rabbi of Salonika

MERTEN: By my own initiative. By a fortunate coincidence, I have at this moment evidence that proves the witness is lying.

ROYAL COUNCILLOR: What happened to the money? You conducted the negotiation by your own initiative. Did you not take the money?

MERTEN: I have stated from the start of my trial that the money was used to pay the workers who would replace the Jews via the intervention of the German "general of the laborers."

ROYAL COUNCILLOR: But didn't you say that everything took place without the knowledge of your superiors?

MERTEN: When the agreements were signed, I reported to the general that I found better laborers who were better nourished.

ROYAL COUNCILLOR: And did you tell the general that you would pay them with these funds?

MERTEN: I could not suggest to the general to send the Jews to their homes. I only told him that since so many were dying, it would be inhuman of us not to release them.

ROYAL COUNCILLOR: Why didn't you do so from the start of the negotiations?

MERTEN: ...

WITNESS: Let me tell you what is happening. Prior to the agreement, he told us on a Friday to interrupt our negotiations so as to telephone to Berlin to determine whether they would accept there the amount that we had proposed. He then told us, "I phoned Berlin, but nothing going."

ROYAL COUNCILLOR: Was even one worker paid with these funds?

WITNESS: I have no information on this. Up until the end of 1943, Jewish laborers worked at the construction site in Thebes. Even today if we go to the village of Karyes, we will see their bones on the fields where the villagers plow.

Never in humanity's modern history has the entire government of a state, all the ministries and all the services, work in cold blood with documents, orders, and protocols for the final extermination of eight million martyrs, as has happened with the Jews. And in this case, Merten, the tyrant and ruler of Salonika, acted with evilness that surpasses any imagination. He promised that there would no longer be a need for persecutions. This only until the contract was signed. Today, on the sidewalks of Salonika, tombstones exist; they are from the Jewish cemetery; these, which he sold, are the tombstones of our coreligionists.

MILITARY COURT JUDGE: Does he bear responsibility?

WITNESS: The Nürnberg court as well as international legal authorities accepted that all Germans, from Göring down to the last soldier who applied the cyanide in the gas chambers, were not responsible for the faithful execution of orders but were accomplices to the crimes—all. Merten, having been sent therefore to Salonika, was the trusted envoy of the National Socialist Party and therefore an accomplice to these hideous acts.

PRESIDENT: When you say accomplice, how do you mean it?

WITNESS: I mean it well. I read in a French book that the Germans had created a special school for the members of the Nazi Party, the "School of the Assassins," a school where Hitler's military were nourished. Merten must have attended this school, too; otherwise, he would not have done all these things.

Merten could have, if he wanted, acted better and against his orders. After all, according to article 47 of the German military penal code, subordinates are not required to execute orders by their superiors to conduct criminal acts.

I subsequently refer to the efforts by the Jews in the capital [of Athens] to prevent the execution of the first deportation to Auschwitz, which had been set for March 13, 1943. When I was notified from Salonika about the transfer, I communicated immediately via telephone that day—it was a Sunday, as I recall—with the archbishop Damaskinos in Psychico. I brought the fact to his attention just as he was about to undergo a throat operation in his house. His Eminence postponed the operation and received me along with Amarilio and Alchanati. After a telephone call of his with Mrs. Lina Tsaldaris, I visited her in Kolonaki, and we arranged an appointment with prime minister Logothetopoulos. On the next day, I did indeed visit Logothetopoulos along with the two other Israelites in the presence also of Mr. Constantine Tsaldaris. I requested to him that the Greek government oppose the deportation of forty to fifty thousand Greek citizens of Salonika. Logothetopoulos replied that up until that moment he had received no information on the subject. He communicated via telephone with Simonides, the governor-general of Macedonia, but the convoy had already departed by then. On the next day, March 14, I visited Logothetopoulos, again with Mr. Tsaldaris, and I protested vehemently that while he was the prime minister he allowed Greeks to be sent to their slaughter in the crematoriums. I also asked him to resign. Logothetopoulos was standing, and he collapsed in his seat, devastated by my words. He replied that he would do everything possible. On the afternoon of the same day, Mr. Tsaldaris invited me to his office and said to me, "Logothetopoulos decided to resign but only after ten days, because the Jewish question is a weakness for Hitler, and he does not want to create the impression that he is resigning because of the deportations. Logothetopoulos did indeed resign, and J. Rallis took over as prime minister. He was approached by the political leaders Kafandaris and Sofoulis and the education minister Louvaris. Rallis decided, as his first political act, to travel to Salonika in an effort to suspend the deportations. He arrived there, was briefed by the governor-general of Macedonia, the archbishop Gennadios, and the chief rabbi Koretz, and he requested to come into contact with Merten; Merten, however, did not receive him, so Rallis returned to Athens.

The Germans, meanwhile, informed about the attempted démarches, kept Mr. Simonides for an entire morning at the *commadatur* and later set him free and then fired Koretz and enclosed him in the Baron Hirsch camp.

From that moment, eighteen convoys with Jews were sent to Auschwitz and Birkenau.

ROYAL COUNCILLOR: You told us that Rallis requested to see Merten and was not admitted. Is this a fact?

WITNESS: Yes. Professor Louvaris, then minister, can verify it, as does Yakoel in his diary.

ROYAL COUNCILLOR: When was Yakoel arrested?

WITNESS: Yakoel was hiding in N. Heraklion. At some point they went to arrest his sister's husband and arrested him as well. They were denounced by an Armenian interpreter named Boudourian.[32]

---

32 Contrary to this, according to the transcript from the collaborators' trial published by *Evraiki Estia* on July 4, 1947, the person who recognized and denounced

A day after his arrest, his journal was brought to me. In September 1944, two months before the cessation of operations of the crematoriums, eight hundred Greek Jews decided to destroy the Auschwitz and Birkenau camps.

The prisoners had obtained dynamite from Polish rebels. On the day scheduled for the uprising, an unfortunate event occurred. A death convoy of prisoners arrived by train, accompanied by dozens of soldiers. No plan had been put in place to counter this new force. Those responsible for the uprising were not able to alert everyone, and so the movement took place only in part, thereby resulting in the deaths of eight hundred Jews.

ROYAL COUNCILLOR: Your testimony, Mr. Moissis, impressed me. It was unbiased and sincere. Please tell me: do you know where the accused came from? Did he arrive directly from Germany?

WITNESS: I cannot, Mr. Councillor, address your question. However, based on my correspondence with the World Jewish Council in New York and London that requested the arrest of Merten in Germany, I can say that he was a practicing lawyer.

He owed his significant influence to the fact that many of his relatives had offered important services to Hitler before 1933. For this reason he was trusted by Hitler and sent to Salonika. Orders against Jews were issued by him as the sole person responsible in Salonika. The fact that he visited Eleftheria Square proves that he wanted to supervise the execution of his order.

DEFENSE (PAPAKYRIAKOPOULOS): How do you know that he had relatives in Hitler's party?

WITNESS: From the World Church Council.

PRESIDENT (to the defense lawyer): Ask another question, and you might get a better answer.

DEFENSE: I am not seeking a better or a worse answer.

ROYAL COUNCILLOR: Do you happen to know what role the accused played in the entrance of the Bulgarians in Macedonia?

WITNESS: The accused invited the city authorities to the Royal Theater of Salonika and there announced the decision to create a political military administration. He was appointed governor and separated Macedonia into four sections.

Yakoel at his brother-in-law's house was Ino Recanati, who, for all his activities during the occupation, was sentenced to death by the Special Court.

ROYAL COUNCILLOR: Whatever happened to all this stolen gold and jewelry?

WITNESS: While the deportations had started, Merten issued order number 5/9888/13-3/43, through which he supposedly transferred to the Greek state the property of all previously deported Jews. The total price amounted to two hundred million dollars. Any such colossal budget would have occupied the US Congress for several months. He, however, transferred it with a single pen stroke. The Committee for the Management of Jewish Property (ΥΔΙΠ) received within a few days a document with the order to transfer all property, movable and immovable, to various friends of his.

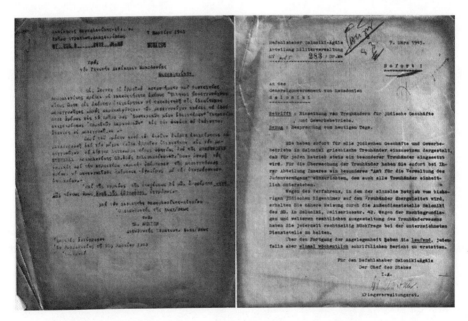

Greek and German copies of an order issued by Max Merten on March 7, 1943, whereby all Jewish store and business owners of Salonika were required to transfer their property to Greek intermediaries.

This situation created huge confusion. The Committee for the Management of Jewish Property wanted to take inventory, etc., and as a result, this order to transfer the properties to Merten's friends was not being executed immediately. At that point Merten commanded, "My orders are to be executed within twenty-four hours without any excuses."

ROYAL COUNCILLOR: So that he would not miss the opportunity.

WITNESS: Something else also occurred, however. The occupation government had issued Law 205, which provided for the process to preserve these properties. Merten's interventions confused us and left no room to apply this law. Then the president of the Committee for the Management of Jewish Property, Douros, visited him and asked him what he should do. Merten replied in anger, "I nullify Law 205."

DEFENSE: Do you have evidence that Merten nullified Law 205? This is a very serious matter.

WITNESS: Of course. They are in the report made by Mr. Douros, who was on the [property] management committee. Finally, I should add that the rescued property amounts to only 0.3 percent of the total. This is plain robbery disguised under a military cloak.

Merten's use of individuals for forced labor is against the rules of international law, apart from the fact that they were mainly fed rotten cabbage.

MILITARY COURT JUDGE: What was the relationship of the accused with Meissner?

MERTEN: He was simply my interpreter, and I did not know about the crimes he was committing. I also report that Meissner was in Greece from 1954 to 1955 and that, during a period of nineteen months, he regularly visited the war criminals' office and confirmed that he was not being prosecuted; in fact, he received an extension of his residence permit by the Immigration Office.

PRESIDENT: Mr. Councillor, please verify.

MILITARY COURT JUDGE (to the witness): Was Merten aware of his actions?

WITNESS: Woe if he, a lawyer, an officer, a prosecutor, as he claimed, had no awareness of his actions. He had a great awareness and acted callously. He was in fact much more senior than General Krensky, the effective commanding officer. Merten's people in Berlin sent Wisliceny and Bruner here before the first destroyed the Jews of Hungary and Czechoslovakia.

DEFENSE: Why did Merten come to Greece?

WITNESS: He was sent by the Furies.

DEFENSE: We do not believe in the Furies.

MATSOUKAS (DEFENSE): Your importance as a witness allows me to ask this question: did Merten carry out any good deeds while in Salonika?

WITNESS: The archbishop and other city officials appealed to Merten to reduce the penalties of people arrested. In some cases he rescued a few individuals.

DEFENSE: Do you consider the accused to be intelligent or stupid?

WITNESS: There are many types of intelligence: smarts can be used for good as well as for evil.

MERTEN: You seem to be very well informed. Why don't you submit to the court the contract between the Greek government and the Jewish community regarding the cemetery?

PRESIDENT (to the interpreter): Which government does the accused mean? That of 1942?

INTERPRETER: Yes.

PRESIDENT (to the interpreter): Tell him that there was no other Greek government then, other than the one in exile.

WITNESS: The issue of the cemetery had been resolved already, since 1936, between the Greek government and the community. Because he was then in the city, Mr. C. Georgacopoulos, the minister of education of the Metaxas government, came to Salonika and told me that this matter needed to be resolved. Because the dead could not be exhumed, we proposed that the location be converted to a park and that the dead no longer be buried there. I do not know what took place on the subject when the Germans occupied Salonika. But even if there do exist amendments to the additional agreement, those would certainly be the product of force.

APPEALS JUDGE (to Merten): If it was supposed to become a park, why did you order its destruction?

MERTEN: The contract that I speak about lists all the reasons. The book *In Memoriam* mentions that, shortly before its destruction, a special envoy of the security ministry arrived from Berlin to Salonika and carried out all the relevant activities on the subject.

PRESIDENT: When your time comes, you can tell us everything. At this point we are looking for your clarifications.

Yomtov Yakoel's police identification card, dated June 1943, shortly before he went into hiding and was issued a fake ID with the false name Georgiadis.

Two of the seven ransom checks. M. Merten's signature can clearly be seen on the back. These checks were obtained from the archives of the National Bank of Greece at around the year 2000 by its then governor, the late Th. Karatzas, after a request made by Raphael Moissis.

Sworn Deposition at Eichmann Trial

The trial of Nazi SS lieutenant colonel Adolf Eichmann, one of the principal organizers of the Holocaust, took place in Jerusalem in 1961[33]. Asher Moissis' deposition was submitted to the trial as Prosecution Document 351, which was admitted as Evidence T/1134. The prototype, written in French, is in the hands of Raphael Moissis.

The undersigned Asher Raphael Moissis, lawyer in Athens accredited by the Areus Pagus[34] and former honorary diplomatic representative of the State of Israel in Athens, declares under oath the following:

1. That from 1926 until 1941 I maintained in Salonika a law office in partnership and cooperation with lawyer Yomtov Yehiel Yakoel.
2. That on March 3, 1941—in other words, on the day after the entrance of German forces in Bulgaria—I left Salonika with my family and settled in Athens, considering that it would be easier for me there to escape from prohibitions and general or personal persecution.
3. That during the deportations of the Jews of Salonika and specifically in April of 1943, my partner and collaborator Yomtov Yakoel was able to escape from the ghetto and he, too, came to Athens and settled with his family in my house in Psychico on 22 Yasemion Street.
4. That when in September 1943 the racial persecution also started in Athens, both I and Yomtov Yakoel and our families hid in a house in Kifissia that had been made available to us by a Greek friend of mine.[35] I went with the false name Alexandros[36] Manzaris and

---

33 Eichmann was sentenced to death and executed in 1962.

34 Greece's supreme court.

35 It is actually the house of Constantine Yannitsis, father of the later minister Tassos Yannitsis, who now resides in the same location.

36 This is the origin of the first name of the translator, Alex Moissis, grandson of Asher, son of Raphael.

Yomtov Yakoel with Aristotelis Georgiadis. The Greek Police of Athens[37] had supplied us with fake ID cards issued with these names.

Angelos Evert, chief of police in Athens, honored by Yad va-Shem as "A Greek Righteous Among the Nations."

5. That before we hid in Kifissia, Yomtov Yakoel and I had visited the archbishop of Athens, Damaskinos, for the last time to determine the outcome of the démarche he had attempted after our request to the German high commissioner in Athens, Ambassador Altenburg, for the nonimplementation of the measures for the deportation of the Jews of Athens and the southern Greek provinces that had come under the German command after the capitulation of Italy.

6. That during this last visit, which took place on the evening of September 27, 1943, in the Bothosakis Villa in Psychico where the archbishop resided, the latter replied to us that the démarche he

---

37 Angelos Evert, honored at Yad va-Shem as "A Greek Righteous Among the Nations," was in charge of the city's police. He was the father of the future Greek government minister and party leader, the late Miltiadis Evert.

had submitted had not produced a positive result and that High Commissioner Altenburg had told him that it was completely impossible for him to intervene because the order for the extension of the racial persecution measures against the Jews of Athens and the provinces where Jews remained came from Berlin and from "very high up"—specifically, from Eichmann.

7. That Yomtov Yakoel, after residing with me in Kifissia for a month, judging that the cohabitation of two families in the same house surrounded, in fact, by rehabilitation houses for German soldiers was dangerous, moved to another house isolated in the suburb of Neo Heraklion and on Agias Philotheis Street, where he lived under the same false name of Aristotelis Georgiadis.

8. That in this secluded retreat he started writing in a journal about the events of the persecutions and deportations of the Jews of Salonika from the day when the German armed forces entered the capital of Greek Macedonia, the details of which he knew better than any other person, given that, as former president of the B'nai B'rith Lodge of Salonika, as legal counsel of the Jewish community of Salonika, as president of the Committee of Social Solidarity, and as a Zionist leader, he himself had played a primary role in the efforts to save the Jewish element from hunger in the beginning and from the persecutions later.

9. That Yomtov Yakoel was not able to complete the composition of the above journal because, betrayed by Boudourian, an agent of the Germans who originated from Salonika, he was arrested on Wednesday, December 22, 1943, at 5:00 p.m. at the house-shelter of his brother-in-law, Moissis Faratzis, who was also living in the suburb of Neo Heraklion.

10. The above half-finished journal was handed to me on the day after the arrest—in other words, on the morning of December 23, 1943—by our common friend Elias Levy or Markezis, director of the Ministry of Social Welfare of Athens, who was residing with Yomtov Yakoel and came to my shelter in Kifissia to announce the arrest and to give me for safekeeping the manuscript with the aforementioned

journal wrapped in the pages of a German newspaper that circulated in Athens during the occupation. I have kept this journal under the same wrapper since then.[38]

11. After the end of the war, Mr. Hasday Kapon, who returned from his deportation in Auschwitz-Birkenau, narrated to me among other things that Yomtov Yakoel, with whom he worked in the Sonderkommando and in the crematoriums, kept notes on everything that took place in the crematoriums, notes that until the day of his execution in September 1944 had filled three bottles and hid them in with the goal, if he survived, of continuing his journal under the title "In Hell." I informed the World Jewish Council immediately about this declaration so that these bottles could be sought and found but have not heard anything since then; and

12. That the text attached to this sworn deposition, typed in Greek and composed of fifty-two pages validated by me and signed at the end of each page, is completely consistent with the prototype manuscript in my hands.

Athens, January 4, 1961.

---

38 The journal along with the German newspaper-wrapper remains in this form in the archives of Raphael Moissis to this day.

The Participation of Jews in Resistance Activities

What follows is a letter from Asher Moissis to Joseph Nehamas[39], sent from Athens on December 6, 1962. This letter is registered in the archives of Yad va-Shem in Jerusalem as item E/1147[40].

My friend Mr. Nehama,

Your brother Albertos, who visited me on the day before yesterday, probably explained to you already that my delayed answer to your November 7 letter was due to my trip to London in the interim.

Pictures: In an old family album, there are indeed small pictures of the unfortunate Nissim Levy and Isaac Angel. I will make sure to magnify them and send them to you.

Resistance: We cannot, unfortunately, be proud of our initiatives and acts of resistance against the Germans during the persecution. This indeed is the weakest point of the whole story, especially in Israel, where the native "Sabras" do not understand how six million Jews were killed without even one German getting a bloody nose. During the Eichmann trial, every effort was made on the one hand to explain this phenomenon and on the other to overemphasize a few initiatives and acts of resistance.

As far as Greece is concerned, my view is that the following historically verified events could be mentioned. In Salonika a certain passive resistance occurred in the form of the escape of about one-tenth of the population either to the Italian-held southern Greece or to the mountains (Vermion, Hassia, Pelion, etc.) where the young Jews who escaped there with the help of the EAM joined the ELAS resistance army.

On our liabilities chart, and it is a shame to mention it, is the fact that as soon as the persecution in Salonika started, the EAM had come into contact

---

39 Joseph Nehamas (1880–1971) was a distinguished Jewish personality of Salonika, educator, banker, and historical author.
40 Abatzopoulos, "Yakoel," page 15

with Koretz and had proposed the organization of a systematic and large-scale escape of the youth to the mountains, but this proposal was unfortunately left unanswered. Surviving witnesses are the Salonika lawyers Demetrios Marangos and Elias Kefalidis, who were both members then of the central executing committee of the EAM.

As an active act of resistance in Greece, one could also consider the escape of fifteen to twenty young men and women from the Larissa concentration camp, where the Jews of Yannina, Trikala, Larissa, and Volos had been transferred temporarily. These young men and women scaled the camp's wall one night and escaped.

The events in Athens you know as much as I, if not better. Acts of passive resistance might include the destruction of the community archives at the end of September 1943, the dissolution of the Community Council, and the signal given to all Jews to leave their homes, obtain fake identification cards, and hide in houses of Christian friends or escape to the mountains.

Another act of organized resistance includes the kidnapping of Rabbi Barzilai by the EAM and his transfer to Karpenisi, a kidnap that was discussed and decided by the unforgettable Yomtov Yakoel, Eli Levy or Markezis, and me.

Specifically, the case is as follows. On Barzilai's second visit, on September 24 or 25, to the infamous organizer of the persecutions, German SS Captain Dieter Wisliceny on Merlin street,[41] the latter asked Barzilai to organize a new Community Council, to record and equip all the Israelites in Athens with special community identity cards, and to perform exactly all his orders, promising that if he complied with these, he (Barzilai) would receive special treatment, as was the case for Koretz in Salonika.

As soon as Barzilai told me this—I waited for him on the intersection of Stadiou and Edward Lo Streets—I went directly to my house in Psychico, where Yakoel and Markezis were located, and I communicated this information to them. Yakoel initially expressed the opinion that Barzilai should carry out Wisliceny's instructions so that we would be in a position to be informed of the Germans' plans. Subsequently, however, we all agreed that this would have made it easier

---

41 The gestapo headquarters in Athens were located on 6 Merlin Street. The location became infamous as a site of interrogation and torture during the German occupation.

for the Germans to implement their plans. Because doubts were expressed as to whether Barzilai would follow our recommendations or the orders of the Germans, it was decided that EAM should be requested to kidnap Barzilai forcibly from his home on 26 Alikarnassos Street and to transfer him to the mountain. Markezis, who was our link to the EAM, conveyed this request, which was carried out after Barzilai previously signed a check to the Bank of Salonika to surrender to the pharmacist Karamertzanis (a representative of EAM) all of the community's deposits. Barzilai was abducted without resistance, was moved initially to a basement in Kolonaki where his beard was shaved off, and was disguised on the next day and transferred clandestinely to the town of Agrinio and from there on to the free Greek mountains. Prior to his departure, informed that I was one of the organizers, he handed over to the people of EAM a letter, addressed to me in Hebrew, where he thanked me and expressed his wish that we meet again soon.

Barzilai's escape upset Wisliceny's plans, and he (Wisliceny) thereupon posted the known announcement of October 4, 1943, and assigned the registration of Jews to the Greek police of Athens.

Unfortunately, a few days later, the Germans succeeded in organizing a community administration chaired by the aging Moissis Bohor Siakis, former president of the Jewish community of Athens, and with Issac Kambelis as its secretary. A few weeks later, after the death of Moissis Siakis, Kambelis was promoted by the Germans to president of the community.

When one month later Yakoel, Markezis, and I were informed while we were all hiding in the suburb of Kifissia that about eight hundred Jews had registered in the community of Siakis and Kambelis, it was decided that Yakoel should go, and he did indeed go one night, to Kambelis's house on Evaggelistrias Street to recommend that he cease collaborating with the Germans, but unfortunately the latter did not comply.

Consequently, we decided to ask the EAM to blow up the synagogue, where each Friday the registered Jews arrived to give their attendance, by placing a time bomb under the registration table. The EAM representatives agreed but, to execute the project, requested the collection of two hundred gold sovereigns. Although, due to our isolation, it was difficult for us to secure this amount, we assigned Pepo Iossif (who survived) to approach well-known Jews, whose places of hiding he knew, to request their contributions. Pepo Iossif was able to come into contact with Mr. Pepo Benouzilio (a survivor), who then volunteered three million drachmas (about seven to eight gold sovereigns), but Levi Peres (who was subsequently arrested and executed), despite being very wealthy then, refused to contribute. After Pepo Iosif visited us in Kifissia and reported the result of his activity, we abandoned the plan to blow up the synagogue. The objective of the plan had been to cripple the Germans' design and to terrorize the registered Jews so that they would stop returning to give their attendance each Friday.

As a deed of active resistance, we should mention the action of a young Jewish woman of Corfu named Minorvo, if I am not mistaken, who as a member of EPON (the National Patriotic Youth Organization) took part in the detonation of the German anti-Semitic organization's (ESPO's) building on Patission Street.[42] Arrested and tried with the first lieutenant of the Greek Air Force Perrikos in front of the German court-martial that met in the "Parnassus"

---

42 Asher Moissis' reference here to the bombing of the ESPO building and of the active participation of a "young Jewish woman from Corfu" who was a member of EPON became the cause for specific research by Raphael Moissis; this is because Raphael Moissis knew that, while Asher Moissis had no direct involvement in this resistance act, the event caused Asher a major inconvenience and very nearly his own life. Quoted is a note by Raphael Moissis published in the magazine *Parathiro sto Dimo Psychicou*, in the March–April 1999 issue: "During the occupation, two Jewish families, the Carasso couple and Asher Moissis' family, lived on Yasemion Street in Psychico near the Skalakia, the former in number 26 and the latter in number 22. Solomon Carasso was the representative or agent of the Adriatica Insurance Company and an Italian citizen. I can never forget the cries of my father of "Carasso, Carasso" on the night of 21 September, 1942. Italian carabinieri had come to arrest him, and he went out to the balcony and was calling the Italian-national neighbor, hoping that he could somehow help. This event was preceded on Sunday, September 20, 1942, by the bombing by the Resistance of the building that housed the ESPO on the corner of Patission and Gladstone Streets. ESPO (the Greek Socialist Patriotic Organization, for those too young to know it) was a pro-Nazi student organization— yes, there was such a thing—that dealt with the registration of the Jews of Athens, and that's why my father and nine other Jewish community leaders were arrested as suspects of the "terrorist" action. Carasso eventually heard the screams and came to the house in the night without, of course, being able to prevent the arrest. The Italians, however, once convinced that the Jewish leaders had no connection with

hall, she conceded her guilt and declared in front of the astonished German judges, when her sentencing to death was announced, that "I was born a Jew, I am a Jew, and I will die a Jew." She was shot to death on the following day.

Other acts of Jewish resistance in Greece certainly exist that I either do not remember or do not have the details of. For example, during the

---

the bombing, released them after forty days of detention in cell 74 of the Averoff Prison, despite strong pressure from the Germans."

The ESPO bombing was, then, not a simple resistance act for Asher Moissis but one that touched him personally and critically, and therefore the somewhat unsubstantiated reference in his letter to Nehama surprised his son Raphael. A minor oversight is the fact that the organization was named PEAN (Panhellenic Union of Youth Fighters) and not EPON (National Patriotic Youth Organization).

The events reported regarding the young Jewish woman from Corfu are more difficult to interpret. One of the protagonists of the explosion, Anthonis Mytilenaios, in his book *March of Martyrs*, reports that, in the trial held in Parnassus Hall on December 31, 1942, two women were among the "defendants": Julia Biba (in an article by Mytilenaios in the newspaper *Eleftheria* on October 28, 1960, she is named *Bilba*) and Ekaterini Besi. The former was twice sentenced to death and executed while the latter was sentenced to five years' imprisonment and survived. In terms of active participation, involvement with the event, and sentencing to death and ultimate fate, Julia Biba fits the description by Asher Moissis. However, in his book, Mytilenaios includes a full family description about both women convicted in the "Parnassus," and, certainly, no Jewish ancestry from Corfu is apparent. Julia in particular is described as the daughter of Dimitris Eleftheroglou and Calliope Psycha from Samos (p. 30), but this does not explain how she came to be called *Biba* or *Bilba* since, in her detailed biography, nothing is mentioned about a marriage of hers.

In the *March of Martyrs* book, a "young Jewish woman Stamos" is mentioned occasionally (p. 128) as privy to PEAN secrets. She was the girlfriend of oncologist Costas Yannatos, a leading member of PEAN who was also sentenced to death in the same trial but managed to survive. The "young Jewish woman Stamos" may be Stamo Batinou, who is mentioned on page 130 of the book *PEAN* by Evanthi Hatzivasiliou (published by the "Σύλλογος για την Έκδοση Ωφελίμων Βιβλίων," Athens 2004), who was also condemned to fifteen years' imprisonment as an accomplice to the sabotage. According to the historian Odette Baron-Vassar, this could be the Jewish woman who Asher Moissis remembered and based on her name, with origins in Yannina and not Corfu.

transport of Jews from the Haidari camp to the Rouf train station for the transfer to Auschwitz, some youngsters escaped by jumping from the trucks. Others also jumped from the moving trains in Greek soil and were saved.

Resistance acts in Auschwitz-Birkenau. I am aware of two histori-cally verified acts of resistance:

a. Herrera from Larissa, a laborer at the Sonderkommando of Birkenau who was working on the transport of ashes from the crematoriums to be deposited in the Vistula River, one day killed with his shovel the armed German SS escort and then threw himself into the Vistula, swam to the other bank of the river, and hid in the swamps. The Germans, assisted by police dogs, found, arrested, and hanged him in Birkenau in the pres-ence of the still-surviving hostages.

b. In September 1944 a group of Greek-Jewish hostages headed by the Corfiot Greek army captain Baruch, organized an armed uprising that aimed to blow up the Sonderkommando facilities. With the help of Polish fellow prisoners, they had come into contact with Polish resistance teams from which they succeeded to obtain surreptitiously dynamite and guns. The day, time, and signal to start the uprising had been set, along with an action plan to neutralize the German guards. Unfortunately, on the day designated for the uprising, a train with newly condemned Jewish prisoners arrived unexpectedly at Birkenau, accompanied as usual by a German SS force. Baruch, the head of the uprising, did not have the time to order those in the other Sonderkommando build-ings to defer the uprising. And so those privy to the plan rose at the predetermined time and killed the German guards in their build-ing. But with the intervention of the unexpected German force, all buildings were surrounded. Those within them, in their desperation, blew up the buildings with the dynamite in their possession, killing themselves along with several Germans. As a reprisal, the Germans executed on the same day eight hundred prisoners, of which most were Greek Jews. During this uprising, in addition to the Corfiot captain Baruch, a leading role was also played by the son of the well-known shoemaker of Venizelos Street in Salonika, Mois Cohen, whose first name I do not remember. Details of this uprising and of the Herrera episode can be obtained from Mr. Chasdai Capon, who was in Auschwitz or Birkenau at the time.

With very best regards,
Asher Moissis

THE ROLE OF CHIEF RABBI KORETZ IN THE DESTRUCTION OF THE JEWS OF SALONIKA

Many people considered that Sewy Koretz, chief rabbi of the great Jewish community of Salonika during the German persecution, facilitated with his weakwilled attitude the occupiers' evil designs. Many years later, in 1971, the chief rabbi's son, Sidney, in an attempt to atone for the memory of his father, collected related items that he submitted to the International Council of B'nai B'rith in Washington, asking for its intervention. The director of the agency, Herman Edelsberg, forwarded the documents to Asher Moissis and asked his opinion. My father's reply clearly did not satisfy the chief rabbi's son and therefore was not used in the data subsequently filed by the Koretz family in the Yad va-Shem archives in Jerusalem. Nor was it included in the rich material about the activities of the chief rabbi that the Israeli professor Minna Rosen gathered and published in her historical study in 2005.[43] In her paper the author begins by taking the innocence of Koretz for granted and justifies the reputation that was attributed to him to the accusations listed in the diary of lawyer Yomtov Yakoel, legal counsel of the Jewish community of Salonika at the time of the dramatic events. Ms. Rosen describes the latter as a man passionate, stubborn, strong willed, and confrontational and as one who accused Koretz for reasons of personal dislike.

As perhaps one of the few survivors who remember Yomtov Yakoel, a fraternal friend and close associate of my father's, I felt it my obligation to try to restore his memory, and for this reason, I wrote an article that was published in Greece and abroad.[44]

---

43 Minna Rozen, "Jews and Greeks Remember Their Past: The Political Career of Tzevi Koretz (1933–43)." *Jewish Social Studies*, New Series, Vol. 12, No. 1 (Autumn 2005): 111–166.

44 Raphael Moissis. "Sewy Koretz et Yomtov Jacoel – Une Contre-réhabilitation." *Magazin Nos Muestros* (June 2011). The article also appeared in the June 2011 issue of the journal *Chronika* of the Central Jewish Council of Greece.

The following pages include Edelsberg's letter and attachments, followed by the response by Asher Moissis.

Chief Rabbi Sewy Koretz on January 20, 1935. The photograph appeared in the February 1935 issue of the Salonika-based monthly magazine I Foni tou Israil.

Herman Edelsberg's letter to Asher Moissis
(Translated from the French)

Dr. Asher Moissis
Friends of B'nai B'rith Lodge
Athens 124, Greece

March 23, 1971

Dear Doctor Moissis,

Mr. Sidney Koretz, who has proved helpful to us on a number of issues, asked for our help to correct what he believes to be a case of injustice done against Rabbi Koretz of Salonika. Mr. Koretz searched the National Archives, where he found material that strongly indicates that Rabbi Koretz was not a partner of the German occupation authorities but rather was a man who resisted the German plan as much as possible. I enclose the material that he sent me. We would very much appreciate it if you could give us the opinion of the current Jewish leadership regarding Rabbi Koretz when you have had the opportunity to examine the three attached documents. I would appreciate a response at your earliest convenience.

With personal greetings,
Herman Edelsberg

B'Nai B'Rith International

The three attachments follow.

Attached Document 1:
From the National Archives, Washington DC
(Translated from the German)

From the Security Police Commander.
Jewish Affairs Section.
Salonika, Aegean

April 15, 1943

To the commander of personnel, Salonika
Attn: Dr. Merten
Subject: Chief Rabbi Dr. Sewy Koretz

Chief rabbi Dr. S. Koretz, currently under arrest, made the following statement during his interrogation regarding his appearance in front of Prime Minister Rallis.

After a conversation with captains Wisliceny and Bruner on April 5, 1943, he realized that the deportation of the Jews of Salonika would continue without interruption. Consequently, he had the idea to try to secure the support of Greek officials to intervene in favor of the Jews. He had been informed on Wednesday, April 7, 1943, that prime minister Rallis was planning a visit to Salonika on April 11. He therefore sought an audience with the prime minister. For this reason, he addressed Dr. Panos,[45] who happened to discuss with him the transfer of Jewish businesses. Panos promised to Convey his request to director general Simonides. On Saturday, April 11, Panos informed him that he would need to be at the metropolitan's palace (the head of the Greek Orthodox Church) at 2:30 p.m. Furthermore, Koretz had spoken via telephone with the metropolitan on the previous day with regard to a telephone conversation on another subject related to religious matters. During this telephone conversation, he had also expressed to the metropolitan the desire to see the prime minister.

---

45 The aforementioned Dr. Panos was the assistant to the director general of Salonika during the occupation, Simonides.

On Saturday, April 11, Koretz was personally invited by the metropolitan, who also asked him to appear at 2:30 p.m. after Dr. Panos had already transmitted this information to him in person. The metropolitan explained to Koretz that he spoke on behalf of the director general. Koretz described the development of his meeting with the prime minister as follows.

He appeared at 2:30 at the metropolitan palace. There he awaited the arrival of the prime minister with the bishop and the dean of the university in a room on the ground floor, while various delegations also awaited an audience with the prime minister in a separate room. After the prime minister's arrival, the others left Koretz to wait alone, and he had to wait until all other audiences had been completed. At that point he was summoned. However, when he faced the prime minister while he was presenting his request to Rallis to intervene with the German officials to prevent the destruction of the Jewish community of Salonika that had existed for two thousand years, he broke down into tears. The prime minister, however, simply responded with some evasive and meaningless phrases.

The description of the event by Koretz appears to agree with the true facts. Koretz was accused of imposing himself upon Rallis without the knowledge of the director general. However, Koretz was infuriated by this charge and repeatedly insisted that he would have never gone for an audience at the palace without the intervention of the director general.

Wisliceny, SS Captain

Attached Document 2:

To the consul general of Germany in Salonika.

Attn: Consul General

Transmitted with the request to be considered.

In a copy that was transmitted to the German chargé d'affaires in Greece, Ambassador Altenburg, Athens.

According to information that we received from a Greek witness, the prime minister was visibly negatively influenced (disgusted) by this scene. It is reported that he told chief rabbi Koretz that it was not within his power to stop the deportation of the Jews. The only thing that he could do was to make certain recommendations to the occupation forces. Subsequently, the metropolitan is reported to have led the chief rabbi out of the room and is supposed to have told him, "Can't you see that the prime minister cannot do anything about this issue?"

This event, in my opinion, is probably not enough for one to initiate disciplinary measures against the metropolitan, the director general, and his assistant doctor Panos. They could defend themselves by stating that Chief Rabbi Koretz, as the leader of a religious community that is publicly recognized in Greece, could not be denied a formal request to be received by the prime minister.

However, the event proves clearly that the Greek authorities, who could have prevented this episode and who could have also predicted that Koretz would attempt to instruct the prime minister to do something about the deportation of the Jews, do not like Koretz. One can assume that they could also have tried to create an alibi for themselves in the event that the British army returned to Salonika, something that they still consider possible.

Based on this incident, which is considered an attempt to disobey a military order, Dr. Koretz has been relieved of his position as head of the community of Salonika and has been placed under house arrest with his family. He will be deported in one of the upcoming convoys and will be placed in Theresienstadt, given that he is viewed as a "privileged Jew," and his exchange with equivalent German prisoners might be considered.

Salonika, April 16, 1943
Signed: Wisliceny, SS Captain

Attached Document 3[46]

---

46 The third attachment consists of photocopies of pages 518–521 of Nora Levin's 1968 book *The Holocaust, The Destruction of European Jewry 1933-1945,* from which elements more aggravating rather than mitigating arise about the chief rabbi.

Response by Asher Moissis
(Translated from the French)

April 2, 1971

Dr. Herman Edelsberg
1640 Rhode Island Ave.
Northwest Washington DC 20036
USA

Dear Dr. Edelsberg,

I received your letter of March 23 and hastened to reply to you.

I have the impression that I am the only person still alive who could express an opinion as it relates to the attitude of the former chief rabbi of Salonika, Dr. Sewy Koretz, during the sad period of the persecutions and annihilation of the great and ancient Jewish community of Salonika. I was president of the community of Salonika in 1934, shortly after Dr. Koretz was invited from Charlottenburg, Germany, to be named chief rabbi of the community, and until my departure from Salonika in March 1941 I was in regular contact and collaboration with him.

It is very difficult for me to express an unfavorable opinion for a person who is deceased and who is unable to defend himself, and I limit myself to telling you that, after the liberation, I publicly denounced the attitude that he demonstrated during the persecutions.

I limit myself therefore to submit to you certain indisputable facts that will allow you and anyone else to form an objective and impartial opinion. I take all responsibility for the accuracy of these facts.

Here are the main ones:

1. In May 1941 and a few days after the occupation of Greece by the German army, Dr. Koretz was arrested by gestapo agents at the Hotel Central in Athens, where he was residing along with the late Jules Tazartes, secretary-general of the B'Nai B'rith Lodge of Athens. They were deported to Vienna for almost one year. Upon his return to Athens, Jules Tazartes described to me the atrocities committed by the Germans in Vienna during the deportation of the Jews to eastern Europe. This proves that Dr. Koretz, already since the year 1941, had been informed of the treatment of Jews by the Nazis. How then could he explain the fact that when in March 1943 the deportations of the Jews of Salonika to Poland started he encouraged the Jews to submit to the orders of the Germans by reassuring them that they would "create in Krakow a new Jewish community like the one in Salonika"?

2. Until the start of the deportations in March 1943, Dr. Koretz was only chief rabbi, while the community's executive power was assigned by the Germans to a so-called communal council under the presidency of a person of sad memory named Sabetay Saltiel. After Adolph Eichmann arrived in Salonika in January 1943 to set up the deportation project, his agents Wisliceny and Brunner invited Dr. Koretz and proposed to have him appointed president of the community. It should be noted that it has been historically established that Eichmann and his agents would select Jews of weak and servile character as collaborators to put into execution their extermination plans. During this period the Jews of Salonika, not trusting the official community administration that was named by the Germans, had formed a committee called the "Committee of Jewish Solidarity" under the presidency of the former president of the B'nai B'rith and my partner, the late Yomtov Yakoel, a lawyer. As soon as this committee became aware of the Germans' intention to appoint Dr. Koretz as president of the community, they invited him to advise him not to accept the nomination.

Dr. Koretz ignored their advice, accepted the presidency, and executed blindly the Germans' orders.

3. When in April 1943 Yomtov Yakoel, urged by me in Athens, escaped the ghetto in Salonika where he had been confined and clandestinely moved with his family to Athens (where he would unfortunately be betrayed and arrested on December 22, 1943, and exterminated in Auschwitz), Dr. Koretz assembled the Jews of Salonika to the Beth-Saul Synagogue and in a speech condemned the escape of Yakoel, treating him as a traitor and advising his audience not to follow his example.

4. Before the start of the deportations (March 13, 1943), Wisliceny and Brunner, wanting to test the character and the physical resistance of Dr. Koretz, invited him by telephone one night at two in the morning to appear at their general headquarters on Velissariou Street and ordered him to deliver a donkey before sunrise. Terrified, Koretz mobilized immediately all the Jews in his entourage to find him the animal and presented it to Eichmann's two satellites, thereby providing them the assurance that he was the person they needed. (It should be noted that the same method to analyze an individual's physical resistance was applied by the Germans a year later in Yannina, where they ordered Sabetay Cabily, one of the administrators of the community, to bring them, within six hours, fifteen thousand kilos of heating wood, which was difficult to collect in such a short period of time).

5. When the deportations had started, the "Committee of Jewish Solidarity" of Salonika asked Dr. Koretz to request to the Germans that they allow the opening of a small hole in the sealed deportation train wagons so that the deportees could breathe. Dr. Koretz's reply was, "I will not go to prison again for the Jews of Salonika."

6. When in January 1943 the Germans started to enclose the Jewish population in "ghettos" to facilitate their deportation to Auschwitz, representatives of the clandestine resistance movement (EAM), the attorneys Mr. Demetrios Marangos and Elias Kefalidis, approached Dr. Koretz and offered their assistance in saving the Jewish youth

and transferring them to the mountains and to the resistance, Dr. Koretz did not act on this proposal.

7. After the fall of Mussolini and the surrender of Italy, the Germans took over the administration of Athens. In September 1943, Captain Dieter Wisliceny arrived in Athens with the mandate by Eichmann to organize the deportations of the Jews of southern Greece who had been left alone by the Italian military occupation. He invited as a first step the rabbi of the community of Athens, Eli Barzilai, who, before appearing in front of him, came to consult with me. I advised him to go and to simply listen to his demands and then to report them to me after his departure at the corner of Stadiou and Homirou Streets in the center of Athens, where I waited for him. After an hour, Barzilai met me and reported that Wisliceny asked him to form a new communal council under his presidency, to compile a list of all the Jews of Athens with their addresses, and to give them special identity cards issued by the community. Concluding, Wisliceny declared to him word-for-word, "If you follow all these instructions, we will make sure that you receive special treatment, as we did in Salonika for Dr. Koretz." What was the special treatment? In fact, Koretz, his family, and his entire entourage were not deported to Auschwitz to be exterminated but were brought to the Theresienstadt concentration camp, where all the "privileged" Jews were gathered.

A rare photograph that shows, one next to the other, the two Jewish religious leaders who played diametrically opposite roles during the dramatic events of the Holocaust. Second from the left is Sewy Koretz and next to him the chief rabbi of Athens, Elias Barzilai, who was willingly kidnapped by the EAM resistance forces and was described as providing an example of passive resistance.
From the November 1936 issue of the magazine Foni tou Israil.

We could add other events that would complete the above. But I think that the above suffices to form an opinion on the person who is the object of my report. We lost 6,200,000 of our brothers, and apart from the primarily responsible Germans, we should look into our consciences to search for the share of responsibility in each one of us. Koretz undoubtedly did not seek the annihilation of the Jews of Salonika, but by finding himself at the head of this great community, he had the duty either to sacrifice himself for them or to set the example of resistance, either passive or active. The accountability of leaders should be sought not during normal periods but in difficult times.

I would be very happy, dear brother Edelsberg, to receive your reply to this so that I am informed of your own opinion on my thoughts.

Fraternally yours

Copies:
1. Dr. E Ehrlich, Bale
2. Mr. Joseph Lowinger, president of the Central Council of Jewish Communities of Greece, Athens.

FROM CHARON'S JAWS

This text is from the personal notes of Raphael Moissis.

Although the German authorities considered the Jews of Athens "unde-sirable" ever since the city fell to the Axis armies in April of 1941, the orga-nized persecution of Athenian Jews and preparation for deportation did not begin until October 3, 1943. On that day the infamous declaration signed by General Jurgen Stroop, a member of the higher SS and a police leader in Greece, appeared on the first page of all newspapers. The declaration ordered all Jews living in the Greater Athens area to register at the community offices and report there on every Saturday. The penalty for noncompliance was exe-cution. Similar consequences were decreed for any Christians who provided shelter to Jews.

Asher Moissis, being aware of the final destiny of such registrations from what had happened to the Jews of Salonika, chose not to register and advised other Jewish friends to do likewise. Every member of our family was provided with false identity papers[47] with assumed Christian names, and we all went into hiding, leaving our home in Psychico where we had just returned after nine months in Yannina.[48] A medium-size truck, overloaded with families and belongings, moaned its way to our hiding place in Kifissia, climbing up and down hills on dirt roads in order to avoid German checkpoints on the avenue. The hiding place was on 9 Koritsas Street, a house belonging to

---

47 As noted elsewhere, the principal role in the issuing of such false identity cards was played by Athens Chief of Police Angelos Evert, father of the prominent postwar political personality Miltiadis Evert.

48 We had previously taken refuge at my mother's family home in Yannina, which, being under Italian occupation, was a haven for persecuted Jews. That situation was dramatically reversed on September 8th, 1943, when Italy's armistice was declared.

one of my father's friends,[49] who gave it to us for free, thus endangering his own life.

There were four somewhat larger houses besides our own in the immediate vicinity. Two of these were occupied by German soldiers, one was a neurological clinic, and the last belonged to the Meletopoulos family. Mr. Meletopoulos was the only well-educated person in the neighbourhood and a known philatelist. All others were good, hardworking farmers who accepted and befriended our family, under our false identities of course. They may have been surprised that my father, an obviously well-learned man, had ended up living among them as one of them, but these were peculiar times, and no questions were asked.

The basement of the suburban house on 9 Koritsas Street in Kifissia where Asher Moissis and his family hid during the German occupation of Athens.

---

49 As also noted elsewhere, it was the summer home of my father's friend Notary Public Constantine Yannitsis and now the permanent residence of Professor Tassos Yannitsis, who was appointed minister of the interior in the 2011 Papademos government.

Ours was a simple place with minimal conveniences and no central heating but with a huge garden where we developed a farmer's life. We raised a few sheep and goats and a lot of chickens, cultivated the land, and lived basically by bartering our products with the products of other neighbours.

One day in early August 1944, my father asked me if I would go to the main square in the Platanos and buy a newspaper. Like children sometimes are, I was not in the mood that day and refused to go, so he decided to risk the exposure and go himself. Across the square he saw a lawyer he knew from Salonika named Toundas. For a few moments, he contemplated whether he should walk over and say hello but on second thought decided it would be better not to. They had no special relationship anyway, and besides, the other guy did not appear to have seen him. So he bought his newspaper and walked back home.

This Toundas worked for the gestapo. He had recognized my father, carefully followed him to our home, and thus uncovered our hiding place.

Toundas, however, was running a "private business" together with two other Greeks who were also on the gestapo payroll. The one, a blond guy I remember well, was named Papazisis. I believe the other's name was Sotiropoulos.

The scope of this "private business" was to identify Jewish families in hiding and blackmail them for money or other valuables in exchange for the promise to free them. After receiving whatever they could find, they delivered the family to the gestapo, thus remaining loyal to both their private as well as their public employment. So, we had the misfortune to fall into the jaws of such a gang.

Toundas's two collaborators came to our home early the next morning. It happened that I opened the door to them. My mother was away because she had gone down to Psychico to collect the food that was credited to our ration books. The food coupons were the only documents that could not be issued in our false names, so we remained listed with our proper names at the Psychico grocer located where the Psychico Alfa-Beta supermarket is today. The grocer, Mr. Barbinis, was a good patriot whom we could trust, so, once every month, either my father or my mother would travel, as secretly as they could, from Kifissia to Psychico to collect our rationed foods. That time was my mother's turn, so she had started out to Psychico in the early morning for what was then a long journey.

When I opened the door, Papazisis asked for a person whose name was meaningless to me. I answered, "No, there is no such person living here." "Is your father short and kind of chubby?" he continued. My dad was actually rather short, but in my eyes he had always been tall and smart-looking. "No, my father is tall and thin," I replied, which confused them for a brief moment. "Does he have blue eyes?" he insisted. My father had huge blue eyes—there was no doubt about that—so I called him. Whereupon the men took their pistols out, took him along to the living room, and closed the remaining three of us—my elder sister, my grandmother from my father's side who lived with us, and me—in a small room that was used for keeping the chickens safe at night.

For long hours they interrogated him, asking for money, sovereigns, jewelry, etc. We are talking about a time close to the end of the war, so except for some real estate my father owned that they were not interested in, we lived on money borrowed from friends. Other than things like my grandmother's wedding ring, there was nothing valuable in the house. They took all that they could find. There was nothing left.

With this interrogation lasting all morning, the neighborhood started to worry. It was certainly not normal for all of us to stay shut in at home without taking any goats or sheep out to pasture. Around half past ten or so, the first neighbor knocked at our door. "Could you spare me some yeast?" he asked but at the same time signaled, "What is going on?"

"Nothing is going on," was all that my father could answer. The man went away but was not convinced. So, two hours later, the second neighbour knocked, this one with the request "Could you spare me a couple of eggs?" although in reality he also wanted to find out what the problem was.

So the whole neighborhood was alerted to the fact that something very peculiar was happening in this house. There was nothing that they could do, however, because, as I have mentioned above, we were surrounded by houses occupied by German soldiers. When, near noon, my mother appeared, returning from Psychico, they stopped and alerted her. She understood but said nothing and came in to join her family. My mother always wore six gold bracelets on her left arm, which were immediately added to the loot.

Finally the interrogation was exhausted, as the traitors became convinced that there was really nothing valuable for them to get from my father, so the time came for them to call the gestapo to come and arrest us. At this crucial moment, my father had this stroke of genius. "Look," he said, "I have nothing to give you, but of course I want to save my family, my children, and my head. Therefore I will make you the following proposal. I will turn in to you the richest Jew in Greece, Solomon Camchi."

Camchi was, at the time, a "big name" that referred to a wealthy Jewish textile merchant. "I will give you Camchi, from whom you will become rich for yourselves and three generations beyond your own. In exchange you will let me free."

"Where is Camchi?" asked the traitors, fortunately unaware that he had already fled to Palestine.

"I don't know where he is, but if you give me forty-eight hours of freedom, I will circulate and search for him. Common friends will trust me, and from the spread of mouth-to-mouth, I will end up discovering Solomon Camchi's hideout."

The proposal was too good for them to refuse, perhaps because they were certain they had nothing to lose. "After all, this guy cannot escape us," they probably thought.

"Make sure that you don't try anything funny," they warned him. "We will be on the watch and have our men in the vicinity all the time. You are the only person allowed to get out of this house; the rest of the family will not stir. And we want Camchi in forty-eight hours."

"But you need to give me my identity papers back so that I may circulate," added my father.

They gave him his documents, and after it was dark, they left. It was August, remember, so when we say it was dark, it was really very late in the evening. The neighborhood barged into the house immediately.

"What the hell is going on?"

My father sent them all away except for Mr. Meletopoulos, and together they went to the latter's home. There he revealed to him first his real identity and second what had actually happened. The other man's first reaction was anger.

"Why did you hide your real identity from us? We would all have been your guardians and would never have allowed this situation to happen. Still, in any case, go back home now and leave things to me."

I return now not to a story that I have heard from others but to a personal picture that I will never forget for as long as I live. I went out to the garden late that night, with the tension of the ordeal that I had gone through, and with great surprise saw that the bushes were moving even though there was not even a breeze. When I approached, I heard this voice coming out of the bush: "Go away, little fellow!"

The Resistance had come down and surrounded our house, armed to the teeth and ready to give a battle, if need be, to save our family.

"Little fellow" Raphael Moissis at the Kifissia Municipal Park, spring 1944

Many years later, when I related this story in a speech at the Public Power Corporation that I headed, I was asked which fraction of the Resistance those men belonged to. The real answer is that the last thing that mattered was whether our protectors were red or blue or whatever other color.[50] The only thing that mattered was that these brave men had played heads or tails with their lives in order to protect a family they did not even know.

At dawn, when the night curfew was lifted, we were moved across the street to the neurological clinic. The clinic, by virtue of being a clinic, enjoyed what was a great privilege at that time of owning a motorcar. The doctor put us all in the car and drove us to freedom. He took us to the area now called Tris Gefyres and to a horrible house unfit for a family of human beings but certainly safer than our previous place of hiding.

The facts just related may appear like an imaginary story to the younger and especially to non-Greeks. They are all true, however, just as is the epilogue to the story.

The next morning the two "gentlemen" went to the house to check that we were all in as they had instructed us to be. When no one answered their knocking, they broke their way in. Immediately upon their breaking into the house, they were arrested for breaking and entering and brought before the chief of the Kifissia police.[51] When they tried to identify themselves as gestapo agents, the Greek officer, fully informed, had no difficulty outsmarting them. "I know who you are, fellows, and I know why you went to that house this morning, but I also know what you were doing there all day yesterday. So, I will give you the opportunity to choose. Option A is that we go together to the gestapo, where I will reveal to them your machinations with the Jews. Option B is that you are kept in the Kifissia jail as common burglars. The choice is all yours!"

Naturally they opted to go to the Kifissia jail as burglars. They were in fact forced to return all the goods that they had collected from our house the day before. And then—now I return to my personal memory—that same evening this brave man, the Kifissia police chief, came himself in uniform to that dungeon in Tris Gefyres and placed the

---

50 Political graffiti in Greece is color-coded: blue is right of center, green is socialist, and red is...red.

51 The lawyer Leonidas Vlahakis, an old Kifissian, told me in the summer of 1985 that the name of the chief of Kifissia police in 1944 was Mr. Hadjis.

six bracelets in my mother's left arm, where they remained for the rest of her life. The two collaborators remained in jail until the liberation and were put to trial, together with Toundas, with Asher Moissis as the public prosecutor. The two received life sentences and died in prison, whereas Toundas was given a lighter sentence.

The fake identification cards of the "Manzaris" (Moissis) family: "Alexander" (Asher), "Keti" (Erietti), and "Maria" (Myriam, Asher's mother)

PART TWO

JUDEO-CHRISTIAN STUDIES

JEWISH AND CHRISTIAN MESSIANISM

This is the text of a speech that Asher Moissis gave to a gathering of the women of the Jewish community of Athens around 1970. The presentation and subsequent discussion were recorded on a cassette tape and then transcribed.

Few are in attendance today; there should have been more. Nevertheless, we will not cancel our efforts and our objective. After all, we take example from the events in Israel. When they decide something, they do not back down but always try to move forward. Many years ago, even before we had created a state, the issue of the fate of certain settlements that border the Arab states and suffer constant attacks had been raised. Certainly, some heads of households said that "it is not possible for us to work during the day and at night to guard the border while armed." But no one considered leaving the village to settle in other free parts. From there came the famous song with the refrain "Lo me leh mi po." I will not leave here! And so, whatever happens, they stay in Kiryat Shmona, one kilometer away from Lebanon, and not a week goes by where they are not attacked at night with bazookas and Katyusha rockets. Nevertheless, none think of leaving their village.

And so with us, since we decided to conduct these meetings and discuss issues of interest to us, we will continue as few as we may be. This also reminds me of a phrase in the Bible, where the Lord said to Moshe Rabbenou:[52]

- I would like you to pray in groups and to be very many.
And Moshe Rabbenou asked the Lord:
- How many should we be when we pray so that Thou are pleased?
- Many, the Lord replied.
- "What if we are one hundred?

---

52 Moses

-   That would be OK.
-   And what if we are not one hundred but are ninety?
-   That would be OK, said the Lord.
-   And what if we are not ninety but eighty?
-   Again, I would be pleased.
-   Seventy? Sixty? Forty?...Ten?
-   OK, but no fewer.

And so we have the minyan that is the necessary quorum for us to pray. And so tonight, we have a minyan! If we find ourselves fewer than the minyan, then we will see what we should do.

The subject of tonight's speech, as you know, is "Jewish and Christian messianism." It is a very interesting topic; indeed, the presence of so many fine women and young ladies here shows the extent of this interest. And it is a matter that has not concerned non-Jewish circles yet as much as it should; and this for reasons that I will explain.

The Messianic Ideal

Each people, as you know, have made a certain contribution to humanity and to civilization. In my view—and it is not mine alone—the Jewish people surely made many great contributions to the civilization of mankind, but one of the most important contributions is the messianic ideal.

Judaism was able to give to a great portion of humanity, even one-half of today's humanity, I could say—if the earth's population today is about three billion (three plus something), then to at least one-half or 1.5 billion—it was able to inspire the messianic idea, which is a purely Jewish ideal.

Of course, as you will hear below, this messianic ideal was transformed and deformed for various reasons, but in its core it remains the same.

So what constitutes this messianic ideal?

The Jewish people were the first who believed in a spiritual God, at a time when all other nations were idolaters, believed in idols, in animals, in natural phenomena. Some had the sun as their god, others the moon, some a cat, others an ox. Remnants of this worship of the ox still exist today in India, where the ox, the cow, is considered a holy living creature.

Well, in this desert of ignorance and idolatry arose the Jewish people, many thousand years ago, in the time of Abraham, and they said: no, it is not possible for people, as rational beings, to worship either animals or stars or anything else; God is a spiritual force that has nothing to do with the mundane.

This God, thanks to the messianic ideal, was adopted by non-Jewish peoples, was adopted by all Christians and Muslims.

In the Far East, where they were far more advanced than the Jews and the other peoples influenced by us, the people also had their gods. And these gods of the Buddhists and the Brahmans were gods not purely pagan but something between the monotheism of the Jews and the polytheism of the idolaters.

So this is, in my opinion, the greatest contribution that our ancestors the Jews gave to humanity; because the Christians and Muslims ultimately worship the God of the Jews, no matter how they see him and what they call him.

Now what constitutes this messianic ideal?

If we read the prophets and especially the prophets Isaiah, Ezekiel, and Daniel, we see that these prophets were very influential and highly respected. They were sort of trustees of God on earth. And they were influential not only to the common folk but also to the governors and even the kings, so much so that they could elevate and dethrone kings.

You may know perhaps the story that Saul, the first king of Israel, was elected by the prophet Samuel, and Samuel anointed him king. From this moment, we have the notion of anointing. The anointment is called in Hebrew *Mashiah*; in other words, *anoint with oil*. It was customary at the time for kings to be anointed with oil. What we now call in the Greek language *Christos* and in the English language *Christ* means *the anointed one*, the *Mashiah*.[53]

---

53 The original Greek text makes reference here to the fact that the Greek word *Christos* literally means *anointed one*.

So this is the start of the prophetic ideal, which initially applied to the kings. The kings, including King Saul and his successor King David and other subsequent ones, before being declared kings, were anointed or, in other words, baptized with oil. It was a kind of "coronation," as we would say today about English kings. It is the crowning, where the king also receives the royal diadem.

The "Anointment" and the Relief from Suffering of the Jewish People

We had the anointment. It did not have the extent and the context that it obtained later but was limited only to the kings.

Over time, however, and when the suffering of the Jewish people began, either in the Diaspora or the captivity in Babylon, the prophets started to preach and to recall the people back to the straight road from which they had deviated and to intimidate the Jewish people and to say that God would one day send an anointed one, a Mashiah, who would relieve us from suffering and would secure us with eternal peace.

Thus the messianic ideal began to assume a completely different, much wider context. And the Jewish people in its history always expected the arrival of the coveted Mashiah to save it from the suffering.

This messianic ideal of the Jewish people, however, has a dual nature. That is, the expected savior, the anointed, the Mashiah, would do two things according to the prophets. First he would save the Jewish people from slavery and from worldly evils. When he was in captivity in Babylon, Jeremiah the Prophet preached, "Do not despair. God will send us the anointed, the Mashiah, to save us from the captivity of Babylon and bring us back again to the land of Israel." Later Isaiah, after his return from the captivity of Babylon, under other circumstances of suffering, wars, and disasters, also preached the coming of the anointed one, of the Mashiah. This is the so-called mundane, the worldly ideal of the expected savior, of the Mashiah.

But the messianic ideal was not limited to this first point, because the Jewish Mashiah, the expected Jew Mashiah, would also have another mission; he would be metaphysical, and he would guarantee eternal peace and free people from their sins.

This messianic ideal assumed a very pacifist content. It was associated, in other words, with the hope of ensuring eternal peace, not only for the Jewish people but generally for all peoples.

The messianic sermons of the prophets predicted that when the expected anointed one, the savior, arrived, all people would ascend to Jerusalem to pray to his God, the Jewish one, and there they would see the realization of world peace.

The sermons of the prophets and specifically those of Isaiah, say that once this messianic ideal is realized, a general and universal and we could also say all-natural world peace will prevail. Then, said Isaiah, all weapons will be melted and transformed into plows. In other words, instead of using guns to kill one another, people will transform these irons into plows to cultivate the land.

Also, Isaiah says that when the anointed, the Mashiah, arrives, the wolf will eat together with the lamb and the lion with the man. There will be no competition, no savagery, not only between people but also among all the creatures of nature. This is the pacifist ideal of messianism.

This messianic ideal was at times much more pronounced and sometimes lost intensity relative to its original content, and this depended on the circumstances under which the Jewish people lived. During times of great misery, everyone certainly read the scriptures and the prophets and relied on the hope that the anointed one would arrive someday to save us. But when everything was restored and a normal and fulfilling life prevailed for the Jewish people, they forgot somewhat the messianic ideal and lived their lives like any other people.

The Various "Anointed Ones"

We see, therefore, as a result of this phenomenon, that in time of great suffering, great torment, not only were the Jewish people committed to the messianic ideal, but many individuals also presented themselves as Messiahs, as messengers of God, as anointed, as destined to save the Jewish people and to free it from the many calamities.

At the time of the Maccabees,[54] when our ancestors were enslaved by the Syrians who pursued them extensively, the messianic ideal flourished greatly.

---

54 A more detailed discussion on the subject of the Maccabees appears in an essay that follows.

The familiar festival of Chanukah is associated with those persecutions—the exemption from the plight of Antiochus Epiphanes, the liberation of Jerusalem, the cleansing of the temple, and the relighting of the "menorah," the "chanoukiyah," etc.

There was, in fact, so much flourish and faith in the messianic power that when they anointed kings and even the Maccabees themselves, they would do so on a sort of temporary basis. Because they said: you are passing through; perhaps during the period of your kingdom, the anointed, the Mashiah, will come, and consequently we should not block his path. We anoint you, we acknowledge you as king, provided, however, that you will be until God sends us the anointed, the Mashiah.

At the time of the successors of the Maccabees, after the death of Mattathias, the head of the family of the Maccabees—the Hasmoneans—and then the death in battle of his oldest son Judah and his succession by his brother Simeon, listen to what the great contemporary Jewish historian Graetz says in his book *Sinai et Golgotha*.[55] I will read a passage (it is French, and I will translate it):

"This power was only given to Simeon and to his descendants until the coming of the prophet. And he was not granted the title of king. According to popular belief, a descendant of the House of David, who would concurrently be the Mashiah, would be the only one able to claim the royal office permanently. The prophet, whose advent would signal the end of the hereditary power of Hasmoneans, was the prophet Elias, "Eliyahu Ha-Navi," who was the forerunner of the Mashiah."

So you see that even kings in certain periods were proclaimed temporarily because they considered that the real king, the permanent king, should be the Mashiah. And all the others would be passersby and temporary and ephemeral, substitutes of the expected Mashiah.

The history of our people met many calamities from this messianic ideal. Because many populists, many demagogues, exploiting this popular belief of the expected coming of the Mashiah, wanted to designate themselves as Mashiah.

---

55 Heinrich Graetz, *Sinaï et Golgotha, ou Les origines du judaisme et du christian-isme, suivi d'un examen critique des évangiles anciens et modernes* (1867)

Sabbatai Zevi and the Dönmes of Salonika

We here in our country should remember one of the greatest episodes that shook the entire Orient and especially Smyrna, Constantinople, and Salonika three hundred years ago, in 1666, associated with Sabbatai Zevi, a rabbi from Smyrna. He had exploited some of his natural qualities. He was very tall, good-looking, and had a very nice voice and great charm.

From Smyrna, where Sabbatai Zevi was born and where he was a rabbi, he started to get the idea that he was destined to become the Mashiah and would lead the Jewish people back to Israel, in other words, that he would gather the dispersed, what we now call the "Kibbutz Galuyot," the gathering of Diaspora Jews to the land of Israel.

After leaving Smyrna, he went to Constantinople and then arrived in Salonika. There he incited the Jews of Salonika by interpreting the scriptures at a synagogue (this a few years prior to 1666). Those of you from Salonika will remember the Kehillah Kedoshah Kyana[56] Synagogue on Valaoritou Street and in Salonika, whose remains still stand as a plot of land and an antique building now.

This synagogue has great historical significance because there the famous Sabbatai Zevi conducted his marriage with the Torah. He held a ceremony there, gathered many of his followers, and presented himself as married to the Torah.

This event made such impression that not only Jews but also non-Jews of the East and of Europe began to follow with interest this messianic movement of Sabbatai Zevi. Even global stock markets were affected; the values of the stock exchanges of Amsterdam and London began to fall as the day approached when Sabbatai Zevi said that the Mashiah would appear and all the Jews would rise and head to the land of Israel.

Of course, the concern even reached the sultan, because anarchy began to occur in the Turkish state as well, and he ordered Sabbatai Zevi to be arrested and introduced before him. Sabbatai Zevi was indeed presented and

---

56 Like many other Salonika synagogues, this synagogue was named after the region of origin of many of its members. This synagogue was named after the Lucania region in southern Italy, which corresponds to the modern region of the Basilicata, the greater part of the province of Salerno (the so-called Cilento), and a portion of that of Cosenza.

the Sultan said to him: "If indeed you are the Mashiah, the Messiah, whom you say that you represent, then do a miracle before me."

Of course he was not able to perform any miracles, and because he got scared, he kneeled, bowed to the sultan, and said, "I accept I am not who the world thinks and agree to become a Muslim." He did not have the mental vigor that truly great men possess when they want to advance, the courage of Jesus Christ who accepted to be sacrificed and crucified and became what he became, the founder of an entire religion. So the sultan placed a turban on his head, and he became a Muslim.

And because many still believed in his movement and that it was part of God's plan for him to become a Muslim, we had many of his followers in Salonika also become Muslims.

Descendants of these were the famous Dönmes in Salonika, or Ma'min as we would call them there. They were a group of Turks who appeared externally as Muslims, although within the homes they were Jews; they secretly performed the Yom Kippur service, conducted the circumcision like we do, and read our prayers but appeared outside as Muslims, as Turks.

When the 1923 Greek-Turkish population exchange took place, these Dönmes were assessed to be Turks by both Turks and Greeks and were all transferred to Turkey, where they now slowly dissolve and are disappearing. Well, they were remnants of the followers of the famous Sabbatai Zevi.

After that, the sultan ordered that Sabbatai Zevi be interned in a prison in Adrianople. But because many people from around the world went there to worship the Mashiah, the sultan banished him to Delvina in Albania, where after a few years he died ingloriously and without a trace of his passage. Only historians remember and mention him, as we do now.

The advent of self-proclaimed Mashiahs followed the plight and calamities of the Jewish people. At the time of the Roman occupation, the time of the "procurators," the Roman commissioners who oppressed our people in Jerusalem and elsewhere, many such Messiahs appeared; it was a sign of the times. Every so often someone would appear, say, "I am the Mashiah," gather a few followers—more than a few are gullible to such, especially when they have their own psychoses—and go out to the desert.

For us Jews, one of these was John the Baptist; there are many others mentioned in our books, while non-Jewish books only mention them occasionally and intermittently.

Jesus Christ: Divine and Human Nature

Jesus Christ was also one of those Messiahs for us. He did not have, however, Sabbatai Zevi's mental weakness. Instead, he possessed great mental strength; his teachings were superior and based on the teachings of the prophets; his successors, the apostles, deified him in our time, while Jesus of Nazareth did not declare himself to be a God.

And for many years after his execution, two hundred to three hundred to four hundred years, the first Christians were divided. Some said that they recognized only the divine nature of Jesus; others recognized only his human nature, and they were known as Nestorians, the followers of Nestor, one of the founders of Christianity; others finally accepted his dual nature, namely that he was both man (a humanized God) and also possessed a divine nature.

Later, the apostles of Jesus and especially Paul preached the messianic ideal of Jesus and established the Christian religion.

For us Jewish scholars, there is no doubt that, without the apostle Paul, the preaching of Jesus Christ would have been limited to the confines of Judaism. At most, the followers of Jesus who believed that he was the Mashiah, whom our people certainly expected, would have constituted a Jewish heresy. Others would have said that he did not have the qualifications that our writings, our prophets, required for them to recognize someone as Mashiah.

And mainly because he did not secure, did not bring, universal and eternal peace, which the prophets attributed to the person of the Mashiah, as I said earlier. And if, when you return to your homes, you open the Bible and read Daniel and Isaiah and Ezekiel, you will see that the prophet must ensure eternal and universal peace, not only for the Jewish people but for all peoples and not only for humans but for all creatures of nature, as I said earlier, the lion with the man, the sheep with the wolf, etc.

So the Jews, when they did not see the realization of this messianic preaching and also did not see realized the liberation of the Jewish people from the Roman yoke and the gathering of the dispersed, did not accept him as the Messiah and still await his coming.

But not all expect him to come. Already a major part of the Jewish people—not here in the East, of course, but in America—reformists and liberals do not believe in the coming of the Mashiah. In their preaching and in several of their prayers, they have eliminated explicitly everything, every phrase that is relevant to the coming of the Mashiah.

This is what we can say about the messianic ideal created from Jewish perception.

The Christian Messianic Ideal

But the Christians have transformed this messianic ideal. The Christians believe that Jesus Christ accomplished and embodied the messianic ideal, that he was the anointed one, the one sent from God to save mankind. We Jews did not believe him because he did not have the qualities that we expected; we wanted him to be our national savior, the mundane patriot who would save us from our earthly bondage by the Romans and the Syrians and any others. And because he did not complete the gathering of the dispersed, for this and other reasons such as the fact that we did not see him as a descendent of David, we did not believe in him as the Messiah.

Well, to address this discrepancy, the Christians changed and transformed completely the Jewish messianic ideal and gave it a completely different content. They said that the Messiah, according to the scriptures, would have no mundane mission but would only ensure the peace of souls and with his Second Coming would also resurrect the dead.

So you can see that the content and meaning of the messianic ideal that was created and shaped by our prophets and our ancestors was transformed completely. We wanted a Messiah who would save the Jewish people on earth but also save the souls of the Jews metaphysically, in other words, after death, in the future life.

The Messiah of contemporary Christians is not expected to do as much. Christians do not ask the Messiah to possess patriotic capabilities.

"Render unto Caesar the Things Which Are Caesar's..."

Related to this principle of diversification and transformation of the messianic ideal is a phrase that appears in the Gospels. The Gospels say that some Pharisees asked Jesus, "Do we have to pay taxes to Caesar?" They asked this because Judea, Palestine, was then tributary to the Romans, to Caesar, in other words.

And so they asked him: should we pay taxes to Caesar? They wanted to put him in a very difficult position. They wanted to understand whether he was indeed also the savior of the Jewish nation and whether he also promised redemption and liberation from the Roman yoke.

Jesus replied with an answer that was of course very diplomatic but did not meet the national feelings of our ancestors. You know what he replied: "Render unto Caesar the things which are Caesar's, and unto God the things that are God's."[57]

As shift response, it was elegant. But it did not satisfy the patriotic feelings of our ancestors, who expected in the Messiah a savior of the nation. In other words, they expected him to free them from the yoke of the Romans and from the tyranny of Pilate. Consequently, those who actually heard his reply ceased to believe in Jesus as the Messiah.

Why the Jews Don't Believe in Jesus as the Messiah

They had other reasons, of course, not to do so, because the Messiah also needed to be a descendant of David, a member of the family of David. And according to the Gospels, descending from the family of David was Joseph, Mary's fiancé, and not Mary herself. Nowhere in the Gospels or in the Acts of the Apostles will you find any confirmation that Mary was of David's race; only Joseph.

But since Joseph was but a simple fiancé and not married and Jesus was born of the Holy Spirit, how can Jesus be a descendant of King David?

Well, this is another reason why most of our ancestors did not believe in the messianic status of Jesus.

---

57 Matthew 22:21 -Ἀπόδοτε οὖν τὰ Καίσαρος Καίσαρι καὶ τὰ τοῦ Θεοῦ τῷ Θεῷ.

And I can also give you other examples. The Gospels say that, on the eighth day, after the circumcision of Jesus, Joseph and Mary took him to the temple to make the ceremony of offering.[58] What is the ceremony of sacrifice or offering? Our scriptures say that "everything that opens the womb, whether human or living creature, belongs to God and should be offered as a sacrifice to the Levite tribe of Aaron." In other words, every firstborn infant who opened the womb, after circumcision, should be offered in person to the temple; otherwise, a substitute should be presented as a sacrifice to the temple. The baby was presented there at the temple, and a ceremony was conducted. This rite was called "the redemption of the firstborn" so that, instead of having these firstborns belong to God, they could become ordinary people.

By exception, the sons of the Levites and the Cohanim were not required to be offered to God as a sacrifice.

So again the question arises. If they did indeed go to conduct the ceremony of the offering—as the Gospels say—then Jesus was not a member of the Levite tribe of David. According to the scriptures, the Mashiah should belong to this tribe; consequently, it was not possible for us to recognize him as the Messiah.

And many Christian scholars today, serious historians and theologians, question the authenticity of Luke's passages, the Gospel of Luke, where he says that they took him on the eighth day after the circumcision to the temple to make the offering.[59] They, too, say, if there was an offering, then how could Jesus belong to the race of David?

What I mean to say is that the position the majority of our people took against the founder of the Christian religion was not unexplained or due to stubbornness or blindness but had important reasons that you would not

---

58 This ceremony, the presentation of the firstborn son at the temple in Jerusalem on the fortieth day, is described in Luke 2:22.

59 Luke 2:22–24. "And when the days of her purification according to the law of Moses were accomplished, they brought him to Jerusalem, to present him to the Lord; As it is written in the law of the Lord, Every male that openeth the womb shall be called holy to the Lord; And to offer a sacrifice according to that which is said in the law of the Lord, A pair of turtledoves, or two young pigeons.

know unless you studied this issue. Furthermore, you may have questions as to why our ancestors did not join the movement, because you are influenced by your environment and what you may have read here (in Greece) or in other Christian countries.

But whoever has studied the issue, whether Jew or Christian, will agree. The Jew is convinced beyond any doubt that Jesus did not fulfill all the qualifications required by our prophets to recognize the coming of the Messiah. And enlightened Christians, scholars, historians, theologians, those who have the courage to free themselves from the religious catechism, also discuss the issue in historical terms.

The Second Coming

As we said earlier, the prophets of Israel had declared that the Messiah, whom they had prophesied, was to bring the redemption of the Jewish people as a nation but also to free all mankind. Yet with the advent of Jesus, nothing essentially changed to realize what the prophets predicted. The sheep does not live beside the wolf, and the man does not live beside the lion. Iron is not only used to cultivate the land but is also used to build swords, to make weapons for us to kill people, and to eviscerate our neighbor under various pretexts and under different causes.

The fathers of the Christian religion, to align themselves with the new situation, began to develop the new, the Christian messianic ideal, a mostly metaphysical ideal based on the hope of the Second Coming of Jesus Christ, the Messiah, to secure finally eternal peace for all people.

And if we do not believe this, it would be good that we wish it to be carried out. Because even before and after the advent of Jesus and before and after the advent of Sabbatai Zevi and all those others who appeared in the history of mankind as redeemers, as the anointed, mankind unfortunately has not known this beautiful period of eternal peace, of eternal love, of the perfection of the human soul.

We continue to be sinful; we still destroy each other on various occasions and under various causes. Hatred still exists between us regardless of our religions. And we Jews, whether we believed in some redeemer or not, have the same deficiencies, the same meanness as other people. We share the need for a redemption of the soul as much as any other people, whether Jews or Christians, Orthodox or Catholic, Brahmans or Buddhists or Muslims.

The Messianic Ideal, Always Beautiful and Very Desirable

It would be very nice and very desirable for the messianic ideal to occur, either for the first time, as we Jews say, or for a second time, as many of the Christians hope and believe. Because people really do need redemption: redemption of the soul, redemption from all the ills that plague us daily.

We see today's humanity devoured either from fears or risks or by war. During our lives, we saw a world war that brought the death and destruction of at least twenty million people. And after that we see the great powers preparing again for another great confrontation.

Can we therefore accept, whether we call ourselves Jews or Christians or Muslims or anything else, that the preaching of the prophets regarding the coming of a savior to ensure a universal and eternal peace has occurred? Unfortunately, we do not see it.

And we would be the first to join the idea of the attainment of the messianic ideal if we saw that the promises of our prophets, those associated with the coming of the Messiah, had been attained.

We would not be so selfish as to claim that the Mashiah come and collect us all in Israel. After all, we have every opportunity already to go to Israel and do not move there but are satisfied to say what we will say in a few days in the Passover Haggadah,[60] "Dayenu."[61] If he saved us where we live now, here in the Diaspora, and provided us with peace in our soul and relieved us from the anxiety of dealing with the constant threats to society as a whole and to each person individually, that would be enough for us.

This, therefore, is the big difference that distinguishes us Jews from the non-Jews as far as the messianic ideal is concerned; the messianic ideal was,

---

60 The Haggadah is the text read during the Jewish Passover dinner, the seder; it recounts the Exodus of the Jews from Egypt and fulfills the commandment of the scripts for each Jew to "tell his son" the story of the liberation from slavery.

61 *Dayenu* is a Hebrew word that roughly means "it would have been enough for us"; it is the title of a prayer song recited during the Passover dinner.

as we said at the beginning, created by the prophets of Israel under a different form, a dual form: salvation of the Jewish nation from its torment, from its slavery, either by the Persians, the Syrians, the Romans, or any other occupier, and also salvation of the soul, so that all of people's faults, whether in continuation of the original sin or not, be eliminated so that eternal love can prevail.

We do not see this purely Jewish messianic ideal accomplished, and consequently we have no choice but to join our hopes and prayers with those of any other people, whether they are called Jews or not, so that this ideal takes place someday.

We Jews personified this messianic ideal, something other nations had not done before us; we personified a hope of salvation. We personified the salvation and named it the "Savior." Other people simply expect salvation, without associating this hope with a certain individual. We call this individual the "Savior," the "Goel." And because the Goel (i.e., the redeemer) had to be anointed, anointed with oil, that is, like our old kings, we have called him "Mashiah," and we wait for the Mashiah. Others also call him "Christ," which also means "Mashiah," in other words, the anointed.

I think I have exhausted the subject and gave you enough to understand the origin and the history of the messianic ideal, its original content, and its subsequent evolution and transformation by the Christians.

I think that I covered certain things you did not know and am ready to respond to any questions.

DISCUSSION

MEMBER OF THE AUDIENCE: I am very happy to have the privilege to be one of the few who listened to you this evening. I have attended many of your presentations, but this evening's was excellent; I say this without wanting to flatter you. Was the word *Messiah* first used by the Jews?
ASHER MOISSIS: Yes; it is a Hebrew word.
MEMBER OF THE AUDIENCE: Because in the beginning etymologically the "anointed" was every king and every liberator, every warrior who would free the people.

ASHER MOISSIS: Not "everyone." First it was the kings. And the first one anointed by the prophet Samuel was King Saul.

MEMBER OF THE AUDIENCE: OK. But he was not a god.

ASHER MOISSIS: No, he was a king.

MEMBER OF THE AUDIENCE: So, when Isaiah and then Daniel add this metaphysical...

ASHER MOISSIS: Character.

MEMBER OF THE AUDIENCE: ...character, or the requirement for someone to be a Messiah, then this is the first transformation. Which corresponds in the end, I think, with the transformation made not by Christ but, as you said, by the followers of Christ.

ASHER MOISSIS: Yes.

MEMBER OF THE AUDIENCE: Hence the first or, I should say, the first two, prophets said that the Messiah will be he who brings universal peace, when the wolf and the lamb eat together. Something that we know is physically and scientifically impossible.

ASHER MOISSIS: Indeed.

MEMBER OF THE AUDIENCE: And the followers of Christ said that the Messiah will appear again when the Second Coming occurs, and the dead will be revived.

ASHER MOISSIS: Yes.

MEMBER OF THE AUDIENCE: Something that we also now know is scientifically impossible. Therefore, they both define an ideal that is unrealizable.

ASHER MOISSIS: It is metaphysical.

MEMBER OF THE AUDIENCE: Metaphysical, which is, however, unrealizable.

ASHER MOISSIS: Yes.

MEMBER OF THE AUDIENCE: On this point, aren't the Jewish and Christian religions the same?

ASHER MOISSIS: Look: on the one hand they do correspond, but we continue to have the illusion that this ideal was never realized until now; the expected Messiah did not yet come to save mankind. While the Christians believe that the savior did come and named him "Our Lord Jesus Christ the Savior." They believe that he came and saved mankind.

MEMBER OF THE AUDIENCE (speaks away from the microphone): But...
isn't this a milestone?

ASHER MOISSIS: I don't know. In any case the Christian catechism teaches
that Jesus came and saved mankind from the original sin, etc. "Saved." Now,
how he saved them, I...

MEMBER OF THE AUDIENCE (speaks away from the microphone): Fine,
this is a...for the people, let's say, so that he could give the people a religion,
so that he could give them something specific.

ASHER MOISSIS: Yes.

MEMBER OF THE AUDIENCE: But didn't the real Christian religion also
move the milestone for the Messiah further away?

ASHER MOISSIS: Yes, further away.

MEMBER OF THE AUDIENCE: Just as with Judaism, it set it at such a
level as to never be realizable.

ASHER MOISSIS: Indeed.

MEMBER OF THE AUDIENCE: And so that people are always waiting for
the Messiah and, based on this ideal, trying to improve themselves.

ASHER MOISSIS: Yes. But the Jewish Messiah also had a positive side, real-
ism, in that it promised the redemption, the salvation from earthly slavery,
from the Romans, if you like, or the Persians, the Syrians, etc.

MEMBER OF THE AUDIENCE: Because they kept the original meaning
of the Messiah.

ASHER MOISSIS: Yes. There are Jews today who say that the Messiah came
in our days, since the State of Israel was recreated and we now have the capa-
bility to gather. Up until 1967 there were some who said that, yes, but the
messianic ideal had not been completed, because we need to take the Beit
ha-Mikdash, the Temple of Solomon.

MEMBER OF THE AUDIENCE: Now we took it.

ASHER MOISSIS: Now that we took it, what happens? We therefore reach
a metaphysical meaning. We can no longer expect the Messiah as a national
liberator, because such a Messiah came in our days. Now perhaps we need to
wait for the other, the metaphysical Messiah, the savior of souls.

MEMBER OF THE AUDIENCE: Yes, but the lamb will not eat with the
lamb.

ASHER MOISSIS: Yes. Then it will eat together, according to Isaiah; then.

MEMBER OF THE AUDIENCE: This will still be taught by those who adopt the Orthodox Jewish faith.

ASHER MOISSIS: Yes.

MEMBER OF THE AUDIENCE: I would like you to clarify, if you would. You said that the reformers in other countries, the Reform Jews, in other words, do not believe in the return of the Messiah.

ASHER MOISSIS: They do not believe "that he will come."

MEMBER OF THE AUDIENCE: "That he will come," yes.

ASHER MOISSIS: Yes, because we do not believe that he ever came.

JUDAISM ON THE HISTORICAL
EXISTENCE OF JESUS CHRIST

My father, Asher Moissis, was faithful to the traditional Jewish religion but inspired by a spirit of genuine religious tolerance. His religious studies demonstrate his attempt to deal with the person of the founder of the Christian religion objectively by relying on traditional religious writings. This position is particularly evident in the two essays that follow.

On the day when Christianity celebrates the birthday of the Nazarene, it is timely for us to investigate the position of ancient and modern Judaism on the question of the historicity of the founder of the Christian religion, as this has not ceased to be questioned even today and even by Christian researchers.

Judaism, as we know, expressed from the beginning objections and reservations on certain aspects of the birth and death of the Nazarene. However, as a religious group, it never put in doubt the historic truth of the birth and existence of the founder of the Christian religion.

Key sources for the study of the initial and primary position of Judaism on the subject are

1. The **Talmud**, written between the second century BC and the AD fifth century.
2. The *Jewish Antiquities* by the Jewish Hellenist historian Flavius Josephus.
3. Certain relevant **Jewish books** written in Hebrew by Jews during the first period of intense Christian catechism and anti-Jewish propaganda, in the period after Constantine the Great, and regarded as apologetic of the Jewish objections.
4. The **works of Jewish philosophers** and historians of the Middle Ages, the Renaissance, and the modern era.

1. THE TALMUD. This book is the digest of Jewish jurisprudence, historiography, and folklore of tens of centuries. It contains the interpretation of

117

the Mosaic Law, the oral tradition which was transmitted from generation to generation and captured in written form from the second BC to the AD fifth century by the School of the Tannaim and by the Amoraim[62] who succeeded them. Many passages in the Talmud allude to the personality and teachings of Jesus, but some Judaic scholars dispute the authenticity of the texts while others note inconsistencies between the Jesus in the text and the Jesus of the Gospels.

It is historically attested that during the period from the time of Constantine the Great until the Renaissance and the French Revolution, when freedom of thought was not guaranteed and obscurantism prevailed, many interventions took place, especially by popes and Western Christian kings, to destroy from manuscripts of the Talmud every passage that put into question the accepted Christian doctrine. Hence it is not possible for us now to be certain that:

a. The surviving texts of the Talmud are authentic copies of the original papyri manuscripts and

b. Whether hints and allegoric references related to Jesus concern the founder of Christianity or some other historical Jesus, since many existed in Talmudic times who bore this name (*Yeshua* or *Yeshu* in Hebrew) and were teachers or interpreters of the Mosaic Law.

Existing disagreements on the subject focus on two primary points:

a. Whether the person repeatedly commemorated in the Talmudic texts (in fact, in some of them with reference and association to Joseph) as "Yeshu Ben Padera" or "Yeshu Ben Stada" is the Jesus of the Gospels and

b. Whether the person implied in other Talmud passages by the word *fulani* (in English, *someone heretic*), who taught during this period non-adherence to the Mosaic Law, corresponds with Jesus of Nazareth.

---

62 The Tannaim ("teachers" in Hebrew) were the rabbinic scholars who recorded their views in the Mishnah from approximately AD 10 to 220. Their 210 year period was immediately followed by that of the Amoraim ("interpreters") from around AD 200 to 500. The discussions and debates of the Amoraim were eventually codified in the Gemara.

Some of those who support the correspondence read in the old surviving manuscripts of the Talmud the word *Padera* as *Virgin*, something not too daring, it may seem at first glance, if we take into account a. the old age and illegibility of the handwriting and b. the shortage of vowels in old Hebrew script.

Certainly worth special attention is the following passage of the Talmud (Sanhedrin 43rd): "For forty days before the execution [of Yeshua] took place, a herald went forth and cried, 'He is going forth to be stoned because he has practiced sorcery and enticed Israel to apostasy. Anyone who can say anything in his favor, let him come forward and plead on his behalf.' But since nothing was brought forward in his favor, he was hanged on the eve of the Passover." But researchers wonder whether this is really about Jesus of Nazareth, since the name Jesus was commonplace during those liberating times immersed in the messianic ideal. According to Josephus, among the twenty-eight high priests who rose to this post in the 107 years from King Herod to the destruction of the Temple of Solomon in AD 70 by Tito, three bore the name Jesus, specifically Jesus the son of Fabus, Jesus the son of Damneus, and Jesus the son of Gamaliel. The fact that the passage speaks about a Jesus who was hanged on Passover eve is, in my opinion, an argument in favor of correspondence. The argument in favor of correspondence is reinforced even more by the following Talmudic commentary in the passage (baraita) according to which "Our rabbis taught: Jesus had five disciples—Mattai, Nakkai, Netzer, Buni, and Todah."[63] In the canonical Gospels, Jesus had, as we know, twelve disciples, among which only Matthew (Mattai) and Thaddeus (Todah) are mentioned in the Talmudic comment, but the difference does not shake the identity argument.

Apart from the specific passages of the Talmud about Jesus that we just considered, as we mentioned above, in it also exist many others of dubious correspondence, which caused and continue to cause much debate among researchers on the subject. It is, however, characteristic that no Talmudic text, specific or undefined, questions the historical existence of the founder and preacher of the Christian religion.

---

63 Sanhedrin 43a.

2. **THE JEWISH ANTIQUITIES,** by Flavius Josephus. Flavius Josephus, the Jewish historian and defender of Judaism, having flourished in the AD first century, records the events related to the appearance of Jesus in passing and in only two short passages of the *Jewish Antiquities* (18:63 and 20:200). The first of these two passages, whose authenticity archeologists continue to debate, states, *"At this time there appeared Jesus, a wise man (if indeed one should call him a man). For he was a doer of startling deeds, a teacher of the people who receive the truth with pleasure. And he gained a following both among many Jews and among many of Greek origin. He was the Messiah. And when Pilate, because of an accusation made by the leading men among us, condemned him to the cross, those who had loved him previously did not cease to do so (for he appeared to them on the third day, living again, just as the divine prophets had spoken of these and countless other wondrous things about him). And up until this very day the tribe of Christians, named after him, has not died out."* The second of the passages reads, "[The Roman governor] *Festus was now dead, and {his successor} Albinus was still upon the road. So {the high priest} Ananus assembled the Sanhedrin of judges, and brought before them the brother of that Jesus who was called Christ (whose name was James) and some of his companions. And when he had formed an accusation against them as breakers of the law, he delivered them to be stoned."*

And while the second of the quoted passages is almost generally considered as irreproachable, the first one has caused and still causes many recriminations. Three interpretations are supported regarding its authenticity. According to the first (the Christian), the entire passage is genuine in its above citation. According to the second, it was added in its entirety by later Christian hands. According to the third and intermediate interpretation, the passage, originally authentic, nevertheless suffered Christian alterations, especially with respect to the phrase within parentheses. The followers of the second and third interpretations observe, among other things, that, if Josephus really wrote the passage as it exists in current texts, he should necessarily have joined Christianity, while it is attested that having lived in Rome past the year AD 90 and perhaps having met there the apostle Peter, he remained faithful to the Jewish faith to the end of his life.

Whichever interpretation, however, we accept as correct, the undeniable conclusion is that Josephus, almost a contemporary of Jesus, considers him to be a historical person, especially considering the events stated in the second of the two passages. The reason that Josephus does not deal in more detail with Jesus is because, when he was writing his antiquities, the appearance of Jesus was still a current rather than a historical event. Furthermore, this event did not occupy the Jewish philosopher Philo the Alexandrian, who was also contemporary, or the Latin writers of the same era.

3. **THE TOLEDOT YESHU.** Judaism apparently felt the need very late to react with defensive writings, projecting its own view against the continually mounting Christian movement. This type of reaction probably appeared after the recognition of Christianity as the official religion of the Roman Empire and the onset of the persecutions of Judaism by the organized Christian church. The occult text entitled *Toledot Yeshu*, or *The History of Jesus*, familiar especially among the Jews of the Middle Ages, should be considered as one of these apologetic attempts intended to protect from destruction the Jewish classes that were threatened by the persecutions, the restrictions, and the sermons of the church against the synagogue. Its date and place of issue are undetermined, as is the name of its author. It is most likely that it was circulated by an unknown and irresponsible Jewish source to be read in secret among the Jews and to present the Jewish position on the occurring problem of Jesus and his messianism. What is of interest to this study is exactly this: the fact that the *Toledot Yeshu* only tries to explain facts about Jesus—his birth, his miracles, and his death—but takes his historical existence as given and historically certain and does not dispute it at all.

4. **THE MODERN AND CONTEMPORARY JEWISH POSITION.** During the long period of medieval obscurantism and religious hatred, Jewish thought was under such terror as to make any public and written Jewish expressions on the subject of Jesus extremely rare. Among the few Jews of the Middle Ages who even vaguely wrote on the subject are Moses Maimonides,[64] Moshe Ben Ezra,[65] and Ibn Gabirol,[66] who also recognize that the Jesus of the Gospels is a historical person who appeared in the AD first

---

64 The great Sephardic rabbi Moses ben Maimon (Maimonides) (1135–1204) modernized Jewish thought.

65 Moshe Ben Ezra (1055–1140) was a Sephardic poet and liturgist.

66 Ibn Gabirol (1040–1110) was a prolific Sephardic poet and philosopher.

century. As human thought was freed and the spirit of tolerance began to discard the old extremism, Jewish perceptions on the problem of Jesus began to appear freely, especially in the Anglo-Saxon countries, where hundreds of books were published by Jewish scholars who, in unbroken unanimity, admitted the historical existence of the Nazarene.

The leading modern Jewish historian Graetz devotes many pages on the subject in his classic *History of the Jews,*[67] making this interpretation one beyond dispute. C. Montefiore,[68] Salomon Reinach,[69] Max Nordau,[70] S. Silverman, Joseph Klausner,[71] Jules Isaac,[72] Edmond Fleg,[73] and all other modern and contemporary authors either see the historic existence of Jesus as unworthy of debate and do not even engage in it or, in discussing it, counter in consensus the alleged objections. Hence Judaism, ancient and modern, is unanimous in the recognition that Jesus of Nazareth on the Lower Galilee was a historical person who taught in Israel and whose teachings were later preached and turned into an independent religion by the rabbi Saul from Tarsus, the subsequently named Apostle Paul.

---

67 See Heinrich Graetz (1817—1891), *History of the Jews* (1853).

68 Claude Montefiore (1858–1938), a British Jewish historian who studied Christianity closely.

69 See Salomon Reinach (1858–1932), *Orpheus: A History of Religions* (1909).

70 Max Nordau (1849–1923), author and Zionist leader and a colleague of Theodore Herzl.

71 See Joseph Klausner (1874–1958), *Jesus of Nazareth* (1922) and *From Jesus to Paul* (1942)

72 See Jules Isaac (1877–1963), *Jesus et Israel* (1948).

73 See Edmond Fleg (1874–1963), *Jésus, raconté par le Juif errant* (1933).

ANNAS AND CAIAPHAS WERE QUISLINGS AND COLLABORATORS

The position of modern Judaism on the personality and teachings
of the founder of the Christian religion

This article was published in the Athens newspaper Kathimerini on Good Friday,
April 22, 1949, and reappeared in the Greek-Jewish newspaper Israilitiki Epitheorisis
also on a Good Friday, April 23, 1976, a year after the death of Asher Moissis in
March 1975.

Greeks and Jews, after their accomplished national restoration, are the only national and spiritual survivors of the ancient world. Both nurtured and offered to humanity two great men: Socrates for the Greeks and Jesus for the Jews. But both also condemned and killed them. And the Greeks on the one hand, to use the wise expression of a contemporary Greek politician, are "collecting" for the condemnation and execution of Socrates, while the Jews are "paying" for the killing of Jesus.

On the day on which millions of Christians celebrate the anniversary of the sacrifice of the Nazarene, the following question is topical: is Judaism as a national and ideological whole responsible for the condemnation and execution of the Nazarene, and what is the position of modern Judaism toward his personality and his teachings?

Let us examine separately each one of these two important and interesting questions.

Those who believe in the Gospels consider the responsibility and guilt of the Jews for the condemnation and execution of Jesus to be unquestionable. Agents of the Jewish priests who were in power at the time arrested him, the Jewish Council of high priests condemned him, and the Jewish mob cried, "crucify, crucify him."

The Jews, wanting to defend themselves against this serious responsibility that is aggravated by the Diaspora and their need to live among

123

Christian populations, considered it necessary to contest the authenticity of the Gospel texts or to interpret these in a way contrary to the accepted Christian catechism.

This hopeless Jewish effort was not possible to bear any fruit because, on the one hand, those Christians devoutly attached to the sacred texts could not be distanced from the tradition and catechism and, on the other hand, those willing to do so did not need the Jewish argument to reject a position that a priori they do not accept.

I believe and maintain that, without affecting the reverence to the holy texts, we can negotiate this delicate issue using historical research as our sure guide.

The political independence of the Jewish nation had been abolished many decades earlier by the Roman legions, and Judea was being governed by relentless Roman commissioners who applied the Roman "jus gentium."[74] The high priest, who constituted the highest level of state authority, was no longer elected based on domestic laws and required to be among the descendants of the Levitical tribe of Aaron but was appointed by the Roman procurator. It is historically attested that the notorious "high priest" Joseph Caiaphas (*Yoseph Bar Kayf* in Hebrew), in front of whom Jesus was led, had been appointed by the Roman commissioner Valerius Gratus in AD 18 and was deposed by his successor Vitellius in AD 36 (Josephus Antiquities 18.2–4).[75] The High Council, composed of members of the Sadducean sect and the

---

74 The jus gentium ("law of peoples") was the body of common laws that applied to foreigners and their dealings with Roman citizens.

75 Josephus's *Jewish Antiquities*, book 18, chapter 2, paragraph 2 reads, "After him came Annius Rufus, under whom died Caesar, the second emperor of the Romans, the duration of whose reign was fifty-seven years, besides six months and two days (of which time Antonius ruled together with him fourteen years; but the duration of his life was seventy-seven years); upon whose death Tiberius Nero, his wife Julia's son, succeeded. He was now the third emperor; and he sent Valerius Gratus to be procurator of Judea, and to succeed Annius Rufus. This man deprived Ananus of the high priesthood, and appointed Ismael, the son of Phabi, to be high priest. He also deprived him in a little time, and ordained Eleazar, the son of Ananus, who had been high priest before, to be high priest; which office, when he had held for a year, Gratus deprived him of it, and gave the high priesthood to Simon, the son of Camithus; and when he had possessed that dignity no longer than a year, Joseph

house of the Boethusians, who were also appointed by the Roman occupation authorities, exercised its legislative and judicial authority.

History records that during that period, constant and repeated revolutions and riots by the Jewish people against Roman authority were drowned in blood. Not only did the clergy and the other Roman-led Jewish authorities not participate in these national uprisings, but on the contrary, they opposed them.

The authors of the chronicles of the Talmud for that turbulent period tore their clothes in despair because individuals almost profane, offenders of the holy law, such as Caiaphas, donned the robe of the high priest that had been consecrated by Aaron. Instead of becoming guardians of the law, they became its transgressors, enemies of the people and usurpers of power. "Woe is me," says the author of the Talmud, "because of the house of Boethus, woe is me because of the house of Anna. Woe, woe, because they are all high priests, and their children treasurers, their sons-in-law trustees of the temple, and their servants beat the people with their staves"[76]

These agents of the Roman occupation authorities had as their only care to flatter their Roman patrons, to facilitate their deeds, and to anticipate and prevent any manifestation that could lead to the disruption of the established order. In line with today's expression, these people were quislings, and if they lived today, they could have been designated collaborators. This swarm of

---

Caiaphas was made his successor. When Gratus had done those things, he went back to Rome, after he had tarried in Judea eleven years, when Pontius Pilate came as his successor." Josephus's *Antiquities of the Jews*, book 18, chapter 4, paragraph 3 reads, "Besides which, he [Vitellius] also deprived Joseph, who was also called Caiaphas, of the high priesthood, and appointed Jonathan the son of Ananus, the former high priest, to succeed him. After which, he took his journey back to Antioch."

76 The relevant section in Talmud Pesachim 57a reads, "Woe is me because of the house of Boethus; woe is me because of their staves! Woe is me because of the house of Hanin, woe is me because of their whisperings! Woe is me because of the house of Kathros, woe is me because of their pens! Woe is me because of the house of Ishmael the son of Phabi, woe is me because of their fists! For they are High Priests and their sons are [Temple] treasurers and their sons-in-law are trustees and their servants beat the people with staves."

Jewish collaborators and associates of the Roman occupation of the AD first century constituted the supposedly Jewish authorities of the enslaved Judea.

According to the narratives in the Gospels, which in broad lines coincide with the surviving Hebrew texts, the swarm of these agents, trembling at the risk of a disturbance in the established order by the public preaching of Jesus and using its shady authority on internal religious affairs, for which the Roman rulers were indifferent, ordered his arrest, which then developed into a death sentence by the same priesthood and into the execution by a Roman firing squad.

The scene described by the Gospels as having taken place in front of the Praetorian, in which the Jewish mob is reported to have demanded with cries the crucifixion of the Nazarene, does not alter our conclusions, because the Evangelists recognize that those yelling in front of the Praetorian were nothing other than agents of the priesthood, which, as was mentioned above, was composed of insensible instruments of the foreign conqueror who had no relation with the genuine popular sentiment. It is well-known that a few days earlier, the Jewish people of Jerusalem welcomed Jesus as he entered the Holy City on a donkey with the cheer "hosanna, hosanna." And one wonders: which of the two represented the public sentiment of the Jewish crowd? The spontaneous "hosanna" of the people of the district or the organized "crucify him" of the Praetorian agents?

The best way to research historical facts, I believe, is to approach them as much as possible with the lens of fantasy and to compare them with contemporary events. Would contemporary free thought consider, for example, the French nation responsible for the executions of French patriots during the period of the German occupation of France, those ordered under the then "prime minister" Laval and executed by his agents in collaboration with the Germans? Is it reasonable to consider the Greek nation responsible for the words and deeds of Greece's occupation "governments"?

A calm and unprejudiced historical examination of the events allows us and obligates us to declare that the conviction and crucifixion of the founder of the Christian religion, which took place in Jerusalem in the year AD 33 under Roman rule and by Jewish administrators appointed by the Roman occupation authorities in contravention of preexisting Jewish legal norms and acting in the name of and for the Roman authority, does not represent and does not burden the Jewish nation either of that time or, even more so, of subsequent generations.

Let us answer now the second question that we posed at the outset of the present study: what is the position of modern Judaism toward the personality and teachings of the founder of the Christian religion?

This position, having traversed various stages, has reached the point today of being almost entirely revisionist. Judaism's initial negative position toward Jesus is dominated by a psychological error. The first Jews to confront the Christian doctrine paid particular and excessive attention to the events of the birth and death of Jesus and, caught up with these, did not appreciate the content and substance of his teachings. The religious controversy that followed and the fanaticism that developed on both sides prevented the sober research and separation of these two different and unequal subjects. People have always had this susceptibility to being influenced by the external appearance of things and by the superficial forms of ideas. Many phenomena of human life were deformed because of this weakness and influenced history.

Contemporary Jewish thought, freed from any kind of prejudice and fanaticism, is now in a position to issue its judgment on the personality and the teachings of the founder of the Christian religion. And it can express this judgment without feeling the need to depart from the spirit of biblical teaching and to abandon accepted dogmas. In fact, what causes a particular impression is that the new revised position has representatives among modern Jewish priests. And these priests, despite the huge distance in time, are much closer to the true Jewish traditions relative to the position of the Roman-promoted "High Priests" Annas and Caiaphas.

It is not possible in a single article to give the full image of modern Jewish notions regarding the personality and teachings of Jesus. I will limit myself to invoke only certain passages from the writings of the most authoritative representatives of modern Jewish thought, clergy and laity.

The famous Jewish-American rabbi and author Enelow, in his erudite book *A Jewish View on Jesus*,[77] writes among others things, "The modern

---

77 H. G. Enelow, *A Jewish View on Jesus* (McMillan and Company, 1920), 176–181.

Jew realizes the ethical power and spiritual beauty of Jesus." In his eyes Jesus takes his place among the noble teachers of ethics and the heroes of faith produced by Israel. He does not hesitate to acknowledge that Jesus insisted on certain views of spiritual life with more endurance than any other Jewish teacher: *"The modern Jew deplores the tragic end of Jesus. Yet, if it was not inevitable—which perhaps it was—it certainly is irrevocable. Some say that it was inevitable, as part of a universal scheme of salvation. Others believe that insofar as it was inevitable, it was due to the calamitous conditions of the age, which destroyed many a Jewish patriot and leader, and ended by destroying the Jewish state...Yet Jesus died as a true ideologue is ever ready to die, with his ideals untouched, uncomprehended but uncowed, with a faith in that Spirit of which he ever felt himself a child and a part, whose sway he had sought to spread, and in whose keeping he felt safe...The love he has inspired, the solace he has given, the good he has engendered, the hope and joy he has kindled—all that is unequalled in human history...The Jew cannot help glorying in what Jesus thus has meant to the world; nor can he help hoping that Jesus may yet serve as a bond of union between Jew and Christian, once his teaching is better known and the bane of misunderstanding at last is removed from his words and his ideal."*

And this is what a representative of the new Jewish rabbinic school writes. Here now is the opinion on the same subject of a modern Jewish scientist, one of the most eminent professors of the Hebrew University of Jerusalem, Joseph Klausner, who can rightfully be regarded as the most authoritative representative of modern Jewish nationalistic thought. In his sensational book *Jesus of Nazareth* he writes: *"There is not the slightest detail in the life story of Jesus, no single line in his teaching on which the seal of Prophetic Judaism is not stamped ...From the standpoint of general humanity he is, indeed, 'a light to the Gentiles.' His disciples have raised the lighted torch of the Law of Israel (even though that Law has been put forward in a mutilated and incomplete form) among the heathen of the four quarters of the world. No Jew can, therefore, overlook the value of Jesus and his teachings from the point of view of universal history. This was a fact that neither Maimonides nor Yehuda-ha-Levi ignored...But Jesus is, for the Jewish nation, a great teacher of morality and an artist in parable...But in his ethical code there is a sublimity, distinctiveness and originality in form unparalleled in any other Hebrew ethical code; neither is there any parallel to the remarkable art of his parables. The shrewdness and sharpness of his proverbs and his forceful epigrams serve, in exceptional degree, to make ethical ideas a popular possession. If ever the day should come and his ethical code be stripped of its wrappings of miracles and mysticism, the Book of the Ethics of Jesus will be one of the choicest treasures in the literature of Israel for all time."*[78]

78 Joseph Klausner, *Jesus of Nazareth: His Life, Times, and Teaching* (Jerusalem, 1922), 413–414

THE MACCABEES AND EUROPEAN CIVILIZATION

Historians and sociologists often pose the question: what would the state of mankind be today if the ancient Greeks had not defeated the Persians at Marathon, Plataea, and Salamis? What would the state of human freedom be today without the French Revolution? And what would the current social and general condition of the European peoples be if Columbus had not discovered America?

And these are fair questions because the events they mention are of historic importance because they influenced the development of the progress of human civilization.

Some of the sociologists and historians, however, add to these questions another one that, in my opinion, also influenced decisively the shaping of the fortunes of mankind. And this question is: what would the state of human civilization be today, and especially of today's three great monotheistic religions, if world history did not include the chapter of the struggles of the Maccabees against the Syrian idolater King Antiochus the Epiphanes or Epimanes?[79]

In a speech that I had the opportunity to give three years ago at a celebratory dinner, similar to this one tonight, and that was later published in a separate document,[80] I analyzed at length the historical events of the rebellion of our ancestors under the leadership of the Maccabees against Antiochus. I will just remind you tonight of these but very briefly.

Antiochus, king of Syria, had seized Jerusalem on Saturday, 25 Kislev, in the year 168 BC, without a fight (because before the Maccabees, the Jews

---

79 *Epiphanes* ('Επιφανής) means *manifest god* in Greek. King Antiochus's eccentric behavior and insanity led some of his contemporaries to call him *Epimanes* ("mad one"), a play on his title *Epiphanes*.

80 Asher Moissis, "The 'Hellenism' Which the Maccabees Fought" (B'nai Berit of Athens Publications). The Greek title is «Ποίον Ελληνισμόν Κατεπολέμησαν οι Μακκαβαίοι» Εκδόσεις Στοάς «Μπενέ Μπερίτ» Αθηνών «Ο ΦΙΛΩΝ», Αρ. 4.

believed that their religion did not allow them to fight on the Sabbath). He desecrated the Temple of Solomon, extinguished the eternal light of the menorah that lit the Kodesh Hakodashim,[81] erected statues of Zeus and Apollo, and issued an order under which Jews were invited to become idolaters, like all people of the then known world, and to abandon monotheism and the commandments of the Mosaic Law. Transgressors were punished by death, and military contingents of the Syrian occupier ran around the cities and villages of Judea and killed every Jew who insisted on observing his or her religion.

The elder Mattathias the Hasmonean or Maccabee, along with his children, organized on the mountainous Modi'in of Judea a guerilla resistance movement against the impious and manic foreign invader. The struggles of these rebels lasted three whole years, and eventually they managed to defeat the armies of Antiochus. Thus on the 25 of the month Kislev in the year 165 BC, the liberator Maccabees entered Jerusalem, cleared the temple of the statues and other symbols of idolatry, and relit the Kodesh Hakodashim, the seven-branched lamp stand of the menorah. It is said that the liberators did not find any holy oil available to light the menorah and were forced to use some dregs of the oil left on it when the occupiers had extinguished it three years before. With that little oil, the menorah stayed lit for eight full days, and the people, attributing this incident to the intervention of Eliyiahu Hanavi,[82] established an eight-day commemoration of this event. Since then, in all the houses of devout Jews, each year on the 25 Kislev, the chanukiah is piously lit.

And so from then on, the eight-branched chanukiah became something distinct from the seven-branched menorah. Because the chanukiah with its eight lamps symbolizes and recalls the *nissim ve nifla'ot*[83] of the liberation of Jerusalem, the cleansing of the temple from the idols, and the miracle of the

---

81 In Hebrew, the *Holy of Holies*, which refers to the inner sanctuary of the temple in Jerusalem. There, during the First Temple, the Ark of the Covenant, which was said to have contained the Ten Commandments, was kept; it could be entered only by the high priest on Yom Kippur.

82 The prophet Elijah or Elias.

83 This Hebrew translates to *the miracles and the wondrous deeds*.

burning of the menorah for eight days with the dried sediment of holy oil, which had been accepted by popular feeling. The menorah with its seven arms, however, symbolizes the seven highest virtues of biblical teaching, which are, for the initiates, light (Oz), justice (Zedek), peace (Shalom), charity (Tzedaka), love (Ahava), harmony (Achdout), and above all these, the central human virtue, truth (Emet).

After this very brief reminder of historical events, we can now repeat the question that we raised at the outset: what would the state of human civilization and monotheistic religions be today if the Maccabees had not rebelled and the will of Antiochus had successfully imposed idolatry on our ancestors?

First, we should not forget that, during that distant age, all the people on earth were idolaters, and only our ancestors were monotheistic and worshipers of a single god, invisible and spiritual. We should also not forget that even Greek philosophy and Roman law had been lifted to an admirable degree of perfection, but neither the first nor the second had declared moral rules similar to those contained in the Ten Mosaic Commandments, which are the foundation of the Jewish faith. Neither from the elegant acropolis nor the strict capitol nor the Buddhist Himalayas had sermons yet been heard such as the biblical "love thy neighbor as thyself" and "that which you hate to be done to you, do not do to another." No Greek, Latin, or Buddhist sage had elevated the human being to the height of the creation in the image of God, from which height emanated contemporary humanism and the idea of respect for human personality.

Had the Maccabees been defeated by Antiochus, the Jewish religion with its moral Decalogue would have been extinguished, idolatry would have become without exception the general religion of all people, people would still be slaves and considered by the rigorous Roman law as things (= Res), and the noble women of Rome would still be entertained at the Colosseum by watching slaves and prisoners devoured by African lions and tigers.

The European Middle Ages, which only lasted five to six centuries, would have lasted without the Maccabees many more centuries, and perhaps our generation would be living in a century of obscurantism.

The causes that shape human history are often random and coincidental. Homer depicts Calchas and Tiresias as blind. In ancient pagan times, the fate of a battle depended on many occasions on the random flight of a bird to the right or left of the camp. The Pythia would continue to prophesize on Mount Parnassus the well-known "you will go, you will return."[84]

The foresight of the pious elder Mattathias the Hasmonean to organize in the rocks of Modi'in a guerilla resistance movement against Antiochus and the heroism of his Maccabee children influenced decisively the evolution of human history, shortened the life of idolatry, dethroned Zeus, Poseidon, and Hermes from Mount Olympus, turned the eyes of human beings to the Sinai and to the Choreiv[85] and thus established the universality of the Mosaic Decalogue.

Since the Jewish people became a full member of the family of nations, since we all came out of the walls of the mental ghetto, we have had a duty not only to light the chanukiah but also to require that global awareness bestows to the Maccabees the position they are worthy to hold in world history: a seat next to the Greek warriors of Marathon and Salamis who prevented Asian barbarism from penetrating Greece and through her the European area; a seat equivalent to that of the attackers of the Bastille, who bestowed to the people of the West constitutional guarantees for human consciousness; a position worthy of all those who during the last twenty centuries fought and sacrificed themselves to replace polytheism and idolatry with monotheism and the worship of an immaterial spiritual and invisible deity.

---

84 In Greek, "ήξεις άφήξεις ουκ εν τω πολέμω θνήξεις." This translates to "You will go you will return not in the war shall you die." This is a reply that Pythia is said to have given to a man who asked her if he would die if he went to war. The answer is ambiguous and takes opposite meanings depending on whether a comma is applied before or after the word *not*.

85 Some scholars define Choreiv as synonymous with Sinai. They add that the Torah mentions three explicit names for Sinai: *Har HaElokim*, mountain of God; *Har Sinai*, mountain of Sinai; and *Har Choreiv*, mountain of the sword. Others disagree and say that Choreiv is the name of the region where Sinai is located.

PART THREE

GREEK-JEWISH STUDIES

THE INTERWAR IMMIGRATION (ALIYAH) OF GREEK-JEWS TO PALESTINE[86]

The Jews of Greece did not fail to respond to the call of the World Zionist Organization and the Jewish Agency for the creation of the right conditions for the re-Judaization of the land of Israel. Thus, even before the Balfour Declaration in 1917, a few Jewish families of Salonika, Monastir, Corfu, Yannina, Trikala, and elsewhere left their homes in Greece to settle in the land of Israel. They emigrated not to die in Israel and be buried in Jerusalem, imbued with the messianic ideal like their ancestors, but to start new lives and to contribute to the effort of political Zionism. And it was not the poor who went to Palestine in search of better living conditions, but, in fact, many wealthy Jews who went for strictly ideological reasons. Among the first to settle in Israel, taking with them their more or less considerable fortunes, were:

- From Salonika: the brothers Moshe and Angel Carasso, Leon Recanati, Isaac and Joseph Alvo, Isaac Aroesti, Isaac Molho, Joseph and Baruch Uziel, Moshe Attias, and David Benveniste
- From Yannina: The David and Batish families
- From Corfu: the Eliyahu family
- From Trikala: Jacob Recanati and Jacob Shalish
- From Larissa: Isaac Cohen and Chaim Cabili

With the arrival in Salonika in 1923 of hundreds of thousands of Greek refugees from Asia Minor and Eastern Thrace after the Greek military disaster in Asia Minor in 1922, the Jewish element lost its majority position in the city's population and abruptly found itself in the minority; this gave rise to a mass exodus to Palestine. The imposition in 1924 in Salonika of an obligatory

---

86 This article appeared as a chapter in "The Zionist Movement in Salonika and in the Other Towns of Greece" in Judeo-Spanish in David Recanati, ed., *Memorial to Salonika*, vol. 1 (Tel Aviv: Committee for the Publication of Books on the Salonika Community, 1971–86)

day of rest on Sunday for all residents of the city, including the Jews, forced Jewish professionals and traders to be idle twice a week (Saturday and Sunday) and gave an additional reason for this exodus. Between 1923 and 1927, boat-loads of emigrants, mainly Jews of the middle class, left from the port of Salonika to the land of Israel. The Arab riots and insurrections in 1929 and 1936 stopped this outflow movement. Thus about fifteen thousand Salonika Jews, or 20 percent of the Jewish population of the Macedonian metropolis, found themselves in Eretz Israel when the Germans began the deportation and extermination of Salonika's Jews in 1943.

On the other hand, in 1921, and by the personal intervention of the late Chaim Weizmann, a group of about two thousand fishermen and workers in the port of Salonika emigrated to and settled in Akko (Saint Jean d'Acre); failing to settle permanently there, they dispersed gradually to Haifa, Tel Aviv, and a few other urban or agricultural locations. A few years later, Aba Choushi, the current mayor of Haifa, sent to Salonika by the Histardut,[87] organized the immigration and establishment in Haifa of hundreds of Jewish families from Salonika; these gradually came to gain control of the maritime city's port. It was the same maritime-worker Salonika Jews who, during the Arab riots of 1936 and the temporary blocking of the port of Haifa, gave a decisive hand to open the port of Tel Aviv, which was conducted by the Yishuv in response to the Arab boycott. Several Jewish families of Salonika, Kastoria, Larissa, and other communities also sent their children to study at the School of Agriculture of Mikveh Israel. Other families, even affluent ones, sent their girls to "Mishke-Hapoalot," directed at the time by Rachel Yanait, the active wife of the late Yitzhak Ben-Zvi, the second president of the State of Israel.

In 1945, a few months after the evacuation of Greece by the German occupying forces, the Zionist Federation of Greece, which had been reconstituted in Athens, was able to collect more than two hundred orphan Jewish boys and girls who had survived the persecution and send them by boat to Eretz Israel thanks to an equivalent number of immigration certificates granted by the Jewish Agency. Most of these children had lost their families and were found in Greek orphanages, knowing neither their families

---

87 The General Federation of Laborers in the land of Israel

nor their first names. Prior to their departure, a special and moving ceremony was organized to give these poor orphans new Jewish names in the Kifissia suburb of Athens, where a temporary shelter had been established by the American Joint Distribution Committee. The president of the Zionist Federation of Greece (and author of this story) named some of the orphans after former Zionist leaders of Salonika lost at Auschwitz, such as Mentesh Benshantzi, Isaac Angel, Yomtov Yakoel, Shemtov Alalouf, and others. These children are now adults living in Israel, and it is doubtful that they know how and why they got their full names.

Worthy of special mention is the immigration in November 1934 and the establishment in Tel Aviv of the president of the Jewish Community of Salonika and the B'nai B'rith Lodge, the late Samuel Leon Recanati. The latter, in collaboration with Moshe Carasso, Isaac Aroesti, and Joseph Alvo, founded in 1934 in Tel Aviv the Palestine Discount Bank, which, after the reconstitution of the State of Israel, took the name *Israel Discount Bank*. The above bank was founded with an initial capital of fifty thousand pounds, and, after the untimely death of its founder in 1945, under the capable direction of his four sons, has become today the first private commercial bank in Israel with one hundred branches in the country and several subsidiaries overseas, including in Geneva, London, New York, and Montevideo. The Israel Discount Bank deploys an international business and is now widely recognized as one of the major economic drivers of Israel. Thousands of Jews from Greece staff its branches and subsidiaries in Israel and elsewhere. Under the auspices of the Discount Bank, multiple investment companies have been established in Israel and contribute significantly to the country's economic and financial development.[88]

---

88 These include the Mercantile Bank of Israel; the Israel Development Mortgage Bank; the Israel Industrial Development Bank; the Cargo Ships "El-Yam;" the Continental Pipe Lines, the oil pipeline that connects the Red Sea to the Mediterranean; "Delek," the Israel Fuel Corporation; the oil exploration company Naphta; the Samson Tire & Rubber Co.; the Mehadrin, citrus company; the Israel Phoenix Insurance Co.; the Electric Wire Co. of Israel; Elco Israel in the heavy equipment manufacturing industry; Hetivoth Hadarom, agricultural development; Philsring textile manufacturing; Property & Building Corporation; Kitan Dimona; Dead Sea Works; Argaman Textile Dye Works; Israel Petrochemical Entreprises; "Shamtan" Lubricants and Chemicals; and Tami Metal Industries.

The immigration of Jews from Greece to Israel took place legally up to a certain point in time and on the basis of immigration certificates granted by the mandate power to the Jewish Agency; the agency distributed these certificates to the regional Zionist unions. But the exit of Jews of Greece and most notably of Salonika to the land of Israel was not limited only to legal immigration and did not always correspond to the number of immigration permits granted by the British Mandate Administration of Palestine. One could even say that legal immigration accounted for only a small percentage of Greece's outflow to the land of Israel. Much of this immigration was carried out by indirect means, of which the two main ones were:

a. The departure to Palestine of the Jews, especially from Salonika, as tourists and temporary visitors. Visits were conducted both by individuals as well as groups. In the first case, the head of the family would establish himself first in Palestine and would be followed later by his family; this was because the British consulates, suspecting that the aforementioned "tourists" were planning to settle permanently in Palestine, did not grant entry visas to multiple members of the same family. The departures in groups, on the other hand, were in the form of trips of society members or pilgrimages for various occasions such as, for example, visiting the trade fairs of the Levant held periodically in Tel Aviv, etc. It is in this way, for example, that in March 1933 the Keren Kayemeth LeIsrael office in Salonika organized a large "tour" in Palestine, using as its excuse the transfer and burial in the cemetery on Troumpeldor Street in Tel Aviv of the bones of the head Zionist leader Moshe Coffinas, who had died and been buried ten years earlier in Volos. On this single occasion, more than 350 Jewish "tourists" from Greece settled permanently in the land of Israel.

b. Indirect means and subterfuge were also put into practice to increase the number of those who immigrated on the basis of immigration permits issued by the British administration. The permits in question were either individual or family ones. If the family that was granted an immigration permit was not large, it was possible to add to it a few children even by the method of fictitious legal adoptions. For this purpose, the candidate immigrant applied to the relevant court in Salonika to "adopt" by a judicial act children in addition to his own that were suggested by the representatives of the Zionist Federation. Under the aforementioned judicial acts, the composition of the Jewish family to emigrate changed and was augmented with the result that the "legal" immigration passports and permits were ultimately issued in the names of real and fictitious members of a family. This fiction, on the one hand, increased the number of immigrants but, on the other, created other complicated and sometimes undesirable consequences. For example, marriages between real and fictional members of an immigrant family who had arrived in the land of Israel in the aforementioned method were prima facie prohibited. In some cases the intervention of religious courts of Israel were required to verify the nonexistence of a legal impediment to such marriages. Unforeseen situations and events created by the fictitious adoptions in question also surfaced after the extermination of 90 percent of the Jewish population of Salonika by the Germans. Thus, some so-called children who survived in Israel their exterminated fathers and mothers tried to present themselves as the legitimate heirs of their lost "parents'" abandoned property in Salonika.

The contribution of Jews from Greece to the illegal immigration (Aliyah B) is also worthy of special mention. Indeed, thanks to the arrival in Greece in 1945 of a team of the clandestine organization Haganah,[89] camouflaged as delegates of the Jewish Agency, more than three thousand Jews from Greece, most survivors of the Polish extermination camps, immigrated illegally to the land of Israel. Dozens of small boats full of young Jewish men and women left the Greek coast in the night and transported them to the Israeli coast. Only one of these boats, the last one, was intercepted by the English off the Palestinian territorial waters, and the immigrants were transferred to temporary concentration camps in Cyprus.

---

89 Haganah (in English, "The Defense") was a Jewish paramilitary organization active from 1920 to 1948 in the British Mandate of Palestine. It formed the basis for the Israel Defense Forces.

The above team of the Haganah was perfectly organized and, among other things, fitted with a radio transmitter and radio receiver for its direct communication with its illegal headquarters in Israel. The above radio was installed in the basement of a house in a suburb of Athens,[90] and its operation put in serious danger its owners and operators due to the fact that during this period (1945–1948), because of the civil war in Greece caused by the communist insurrection, possession of a radio transmitter was punishable with the death penalty. The Hellenic authorities, favoring the departure of Jews from Greece, were indifferent to the activities of the Haganah team, and in the rare instances when they intervened, they did so only under pressure from the British military mission in Athens and its Intelligence Service. Following one such British intervention in 1947, Greece's minister of interior suspended from his post for six months Mr. Dimitris Vlastaris, the director general of Alien Services and Information. In another similar case, the Court of Piraeus fined two members of the Haganah for coordinating the illegal exit of some young Jews without passports. It should also be noted that the Haganah team maintained during this period, in the region of Galatsi in the outskirts of Athens, an agricultural training center (Hashahar) for the young Jews whom it secretly channeled successively and clandestinely from the Greek to the Palestinian coast. And it was not only Jews from Greece who were channeled in this way to Israel but also Jews who were brought to Greece from central Europe, most notably from Hungary. Heading this mission was Mr. Jacob Tzur (Tzernovitz), the current chairman of the board of directors of Keren Kayemeth LeIsrael, who stayed for several months in Athens and also facilitated the reorganization of the Zionist movement in Greece after World War II. Following his return to Israel, he was replaced by Mr. Elyihau Shachnay of Haifa.

---

90 He does not state it in the article, but the basement was actually in Asher Moissis' own house! While the English translation of this text was being prepared, the translator (Alex Moissis, grandson of Asher) and the editor (his father, Raphael Moissis) had the following exchange via e-mail:

TRANSLATOR: Do you have any idea in which basement the radio transmitter and receiver of the Haganah may have been placed? The author of the article seems to have intimate knowledge of the clandestine operations of the second aliyah.

EDITOR: I had forgotten about it, but, as Maurice Chevalier sang in Gigi, "Yes. I remember it well!" It became the family radio for several years after completing its clandestine role.

LEON RECANATI AND I

This text was translated from a typewritten French text by Asher Moissis entitled "Leon Recanati et Moi." The value of the text is that it contains anecdotes, personal information, and impressions from the author.

If someone wants to study the historical events in the twentieth century that preceded the ruin and effective destruction of the Jewish community of Salonika, the existence of which lasted for about four centuries, he or she must focus on three major events that contributed to the extinction of this community. These three events are

1. The great fire of August 6, 1917, in this large and enviable Macedonian capital, which in a single night turned into rubble about 70 percent of the Jewish homes and business premises.
2. The installation in 1922 and 1923 of more than two hundred thousand new residents, Greek refugees from Asia Minor and Western Thrace, an installation that overturned the demographic composition and transformed the hitherto-majority Jewish element into a minority.
3. The German racial persecution of the year 1943 that eliminated 96 percent of the city's Jewish population.

The great fire of 1917 preceded by three short months the Balfour Declaration of November 2, 1917, and so the Jews of Salonika did not have the time to be influenced by the statement and turn their gaze to the still-deserted land of Israel. Instead, some twenty thousand Salonika Jews migrated to Paris,[91] and only a few dozen turned to the land of Israel. A more

---

91 Among those who migrated to Paris at the time was Bénédict Mallah, born Aaron "Beniko" Mallah, grandfather of France's later president Nicolas Sarkozy. Mallah was born in Salonika in 1890.

decisive influence, in terms of the migration flow and the preference for the land of Israel, was the massive establishment in Salonika as of the year 1922 of Greek refugees originating from Asia Minor and Thrace.[92]

In one of his speeches in London, the former president of the World Zionist Organization Dr. Chaim Weizmann had said that each one of these Greek refugees prompted inevitably the transfer of two Jewish inhabitants of Salonika. Indeed, and without allowing for any other motive, this sharp demographic and economic compression between the old and new inhabitants of the city led to the exit of about twenty thousand of the less affluent of the city's Jews to the land of Israel.

At the outset of the Second World War, about fifty thousand Jews, remained in Salonica of whom forty-five thousand were to be transferred to and to die in Auschwitz and Bergen-Belsen while not more than five thousand were able to return.

The Jewish community of Salonika from the period of the fire of the year 1917 until the persecution of 1943 resembled a seriously ill organism of which doctors did not predict much hope of survival. But as ill patients often show in their last moments some signs of improving health, during the last twenty-five years of the life of the Jewish community of Salonika, there had been some signs of vitality and action. The new Jewish generation, well educated, multilingual, and imbued by modern ideas, had started to affect community life and produced distinguished personalities that had

---

92 Salonika was part of the Ottoman Empire until 1912. On October 26, 1912, the Greek army, under the leadership of the prince and future king Constantine, entered the city. As Salonika joined Greece as the young kingdom's second-largest city, the mostly Sephardic and Spanish-speaking (Ladino) Jewish population became Greek citizens. The community's need to adapt and to protect its rights within the Greek nation-state created professional opportunities for Jews such as Asher Moissis, who was familiar with the Greek administration and laws. Asher Moissis had both Romaniote as well as Sephardic parents and was thus fluent in both Greek and Ladino. Furthermore, after growing up in the town of Trikala in central Greece, he studied law at the National University of Athens and passed the bar examinations by the Greek Supreme Court, the Areus Pagus. As a practicing Greek attorney fluent in both Greek and Ladino, he then moved to Salonika and set up his office there, along with his partner, Yomtov Yakoel, who had similar origins and a similar background.

not existed in previous generations. Within this new ruling class and among these personalities was without doubt Leon Samuel Recanati.

I had met Leon Recanati many years earlier when he was still the director of the Salonika tobacco company Fumare. But my collaboration with him did not start until 1929 when, at the assembly of representatives of the Jewish communities of Greece that convened that year in Salonika, he was elected representative of Greek Jewry to the World Jewish Congress, which was held in London to establish the Jewish Agency for the Liberation of Palestine. I was one of the main organizers and speakers at that assembly, and, despite my young age, I participated in the twelve-member Communal Board and had already started to play a role disproportionate to my age in Jewish public life. Consequently I had influenced somewhat the members of the assembly in favor of Leon Recanati's election, because, from the gatherings of the B'nai B'rith Lodge of Salonika where he and I were ordinary members, I had particularly appreciated his skills, his character, and his healthy and pure thinking.

An undated coin and a 1985 stamp that were issued in Israel to commemorate Leon Recanati.

Leon Recanati's election constituted an important new development because, apart from him, there were other prominent candidates, including Senator Asher Mallah, the famous journalist and orator Mendesh Bessagni,

145

the veteran and ardent Zionist David Florentin, and others who already had on their records substantial public activity and every right to claim this honor.

I had felt deep satisfaction when, after his unanimous election by the assembly, Leon Recanati ascended to the podium and, with great emotion, delivered his prepared speech overflowing with Jewish sentiments and philosophical thoughts, which impressed the members of assembly. It can be said that his election marked the beginning of the public career of Leon Recanati in the Jewish community of Salonika, which had still been substantial then.

In 1930, general elections were held to renew the seventy-member General Communal Assembly, the highest authority of the Jewish community of Salonika. Due to his personal skills and the confidence that it held in his Zionist feelings, the Zionist Federation of Greece registered Leon Recanati on its list of candidates as an "independent." As a member of the General Communal Assembly, Leon Recanati had the opportunity to demonstrate publicly his dynamic personality and organizational skills. Thanks to these he was elected shortly thereafter president of the B'nai B'rith Lodge of Salonika, which at the time enjoyed great prestige and was a key element in the public life of Jewish Salonika. Leon Recanati's strong personality, dynamism, and moderation contributed to the further enhancement of the prestige and influence of the B'nai B'rith Lodge in the eyes of Jews and Greeks and to an increase in its membership.

Shortly after his election as president of the lodge and then in 1934 the immigration to Israel of David Florentin, the veteran Zionist vice president of the lodge, I was elected to the latter's position and henceforth began to collaborate more directly with Leon Recanati.

During Leon Recanati's presidency at the lodge, the sad incidents that were called "the Campbell events" occurred in Salonika. These shook the lives of the Jews of Salonika and disturbed not only the latter but also a large part of the Greek public that did not endorse them. The reader can find details of these unfortunate events and their causes in my work "History of the Zionist Movement in Greece," which was published in one of my other books.[93] I should add here that during those difficult times, Leon Recanati

---

93 In June of 1931, Greek anti-Semitic gangs took to the streets of Salonika threatening the Jewish inhabitants. Quoting from *Greece: A Jewish History* by K.E. Fleming

was one of the major developers of the defense of the Jewish position, and his measured and wise advice was always heard with care.

Leon Recanati's office on Agiou Mina Street was converted during that time into a center of Jewish self-defense, and among the many people who frequented the place daily was the unforgettable Guerson Agronsky (Agron), who had arrived in Salonika as special envoy of the *London Times* newspaper to cover the tragic events and who, after the establishment of the State of Israel, served as mayor of Jerusalem. If Guerson Agronsky were alive today, he would have much to recount regarding Leon Recanati's boundless activity in that difficult situation. I remember that, when calm was restored in the city of Salonika, Recanati confided to me that the riots had so puzzled him that he decided to immigrate to the land of Israel, a migration he carried out in late 1934.

In 1933 new elections were held for the renewal of the seventy-member Community Assembly of the Jewish community of Salonika. In these elections about twelve thousand Jews aged over twenty-one voted, not including women, who did not yet have voting rights in Greece. Even though the proportional electoral system was in effect, the Zionists received the absolute majority and thus assumed the responsibility of creating the Community Council. Leon Recanati was elected president of the community and I vice president. Consequently, our cooperation within the framework of the B'nai B'rith Lodge was also extended to community affairs. The general view was that the new City Council was the best that the community had had in recent years, since it inaugurated a new spirit, introduced new methods for

---

(2008), "On June 29, [the newspaper] *Makedonia*'s oversize headline urged its readers to 'Finish [the Jews] Off!' That night, a crowd numbering in the thousands set fire to the heavily Jewish 'Campbell' district, a poor area where Jewish refugees of the 1917 fire had resettled in dwellings that were little more than huts. Quickly, the violence spread to other districts as well, with synagogues laid siege, houses burned and looted, and Jewish property destroyed across the city. [Greek prime minister] Venizelos now moved swiftly: he delegated government officials to meet with the Jewish leader, and reiterated to Parliament that 'the attacks on the Jews were lamentable and without justification.' Martial law was declared, and an army battalion was sent to protect Salonika's Jewish neighborhoods." Asher Moissis' own account of this incident, as an eyewitness, appears later in this book.

the management of community affairs, staffed municipal committees with young men with modern ideas, and generally succeeded in revamping the entire communal structure.

When in late November 1934 Leon Recanati left Salonika definitively and settled in Tel Aviv, the City Council, on his recommendation, elected me as president of the community; I did my best to continue the work, the modernization program, and the renewal. My task was more difficult due to my age (I was then thirty-four years old) and due to the fact that I had neither the prestige nor the economic independence that my distinguished predecessor enjoyed.

We had departed together from Salonika to Israel on November 4, 1934, I by sea on the ship *Tevere*[94] and he by rail through Turkey and Syria because he did not manage marine transport well. We met a few days later in Tel Aviv, which at that time had about forty thousand residents. There, Leon Recanati along with our compatriots Moshe Carasso, Joseph Alvo, and Isaac Aroesti agreed to establish a new banking firm under the name of *Palestine Discount Bank*.

LLOYD TRIESTINO   P.fo « TEVERE »

The steamship Tevere on which Asher Moissis travelled from Salonika to Israel in 1934.

---

94 *Gablonz*, built in 1912 for Lloyd Austriaco, was transferred in 1919 to Lloyd Triestino. In 1921 it was renamed *Tevere*. On January 17, 1943, *Tevere* was scuttled at Tripoli after mine damage. Source: http://www.wrecksite.eu/wreck.aspx?143338.

For this purpose Recanati rented a small apartment on the ground floor of a building on Jehuda Halevy Street in Tel Aviv, and his first care was to deposit the minimum capital of fifty thousand Palestinian pounds required by Palestinian law. For the record, I should point out that Leon Recanati's decision to immigrate to and settle in the land of Israel in 1934 was due solely to ideological and emotional reasons, as he had abandoned in Salonika a highly prosperous commercial tobacco company.

However, Leon Recanati's interest for his compatriots in Salonika and their problems did not stop after his establishment in Tel Aviv.

From the time of his departure until the outbreak of the Second World War, he visited the city of Salonika once or twice, and during those visits he participated in the meetings of the Community Council, the Directorate of the Zionist Federation of Greece, and other Jewish organizations so that he could be informed about the issues they were dealing with and offer his advice and support. During the period of the German occupation and the racial persecutions in Greece, Leon Recanati conducted vigorous activities to rescue his endangered compatriots and was the originator of the decision by the Agence Juive for Palestine to secretly charter a small boat that occasionally effected illegally the trip from the small port of Tsakei of the community of Mesochori in the province of Karystos on the east coast of the Greek island of Euboea to the Turkish port of Chesme of Smyrna and transferred hundreds of persecuted Jews to the land of Israel. In addition to this, using the same route, several hundred Greek officers escaped from Greece to join and strengthen the forces of the Greek army that was being reorganized in the land of Israel and in Egypt.

The town of Tsakei near Mesochori on the island of Euboea. Jewish and other refugees boarded boats in the small nearby harbor to escape the German occupation and to head to Palestine and Egypt via Turkey.

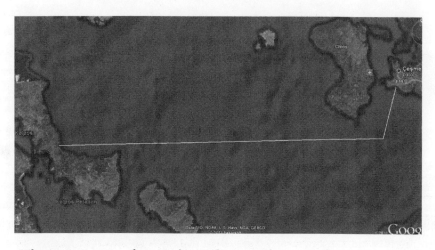

The Aegean crossing from Tsakei, Euboea, to Chesme, Turkey (a distance of around 120 miles {195 km}).

To the refugees who succeeded to arrive in Tel Aviv, Leon Recanati granted personally and with the mediation of the Palestine Discount Bank loans and grants to meet their challenges. Leon Recanati also provided his moral and material support for the development in Tel Aviv, at the location where Yad Eliyahu exists today, of the Shikoun Ole Yavan, which offered housing to the refugees arriving from Greece.

To the initiative and efforts of Leon Recanati, Asher Mallah, and other Zionist figures living in the land of Israel should also be attributed the rapprochement made by the Agence Juive with the British military authorities to reach agreement for the exchange of a dozen Zionist leaders of Salonika for German officers who were prisoners of war. This exchange did not take place in the end because in the meantime the Zionist leaders had been displaced and exterminated at Auschwitz or had joined the resistance, as was the case for myself, Robert Raphael, and Solomon Bity.

Finally, I mention two painful memories of my last contacts with my unforgettable friend Leon Recanati. The first refers to a message he sent me in Athens through the intermediation of the International Red Cross in early 1943 when the deportations of Jews to Auschwitz had begun in Salonika. In that message he asked me for news about the condition of his compatriots.

Unable to reply openly and to describe the actual situation because of the strict censorship of the Germans, I restricted myself to reply with the following laconic words: "All here and in Salonika enjoy good health. Your father is even better." The answer was, of course, very significant for Leon Recanati since his father had died long before the war, and so my correspondent understood very well what I wanted to say without the Germans realizing the true meaning of my response. My second memory relates to the first telegram I received in Athens from Leon Recanati from Tel Aviv in November 1944, as soon as he learned from the Intelligence Service that I had survived the persecutions and was located in Athens. In his telegram he asked for news about the fate of our compatriots and friends who had been displaced to Auschwitz. My answer was of course disappointing and spread general mourning to all our compatriots who lived in the land of Israel and had had the good fortune to leave Salonika before the war and the persecutions.

THE SALONIKA MACCABI TEAM AND THE "CAMPBELL" INCIDENT OF 1931[95]

The founders and early leaders of the Zionist movement had full knowledge that the rebirth of the Jewish people could not be achieved without the revival of Jewish youth. The ancient Greek saying "a healthy mind in a healthy body" has parallel equivalents in the Proverbs and the Talmud. In this context, Zionism began an effort to promote athletics among Jewish youth. Those in the Diaspora who lived during the Middle Ages in closed and obscure ghettos had neglected any care of the human body. This effort was undertaken specifically by the Maccabi World Union, founded in 1895[96] with headquarters first in Berlin and later in London. According to its statutes, the purpose of this organization was the "spiritual and physical education of its members so that they can participate responsibly in any national effort by the Jewish people and especially in the reconstruction of the land of Israel." After its foundation, regional athletic unions under the name *Maccabi* were gradually created in all countries where Jews lived, including, of course, Palestine.

In Salonika the first "Maccabi" athletic union was founded in 1908 on the occasion of the arrival on that date in the city of the Maccabi Athletic Union of Philipopolis, the capital of Eastern Rumelia, to participate in the festivities for the first anniversary of the proclamation of the Turkish Constitution. The foundation act and the approval of its statutes took place on December 12, 1908. Within a small period of time, about a hundred young Jews joined this union, which began to organize gym courses first in the courtyard of the

---

95 This article appeared as a chapter in "The Zionist Movement in Salonika and in the Other Towns of Greece" in Judeo-Spanish in David Recanati, ed., *Memorial to Salonika*, vol. 1 (Tel Aviv: Committee for the Publication of Books on the Salonika Community, 1971–86).

96 The Maccabi World Union was actually created at the Twelfth World Zionist Congress in Carlsbad (Karlovy Vary, Czechoslovakia) in 1921 as an umbrella organization to combine all prior Zionist athletic clubs. The earliest such club, founded in 1895 in Constantinople, was the Israelite Gymnastic Association Constantinople.

Alcheh Jewish High School and later at the "Talmud Torah Agadol" communal school. In 1912 the number of young members of the Salonika Maccabi exceeded three hundred. The club employed as its coach the gym instructor of the Turkish army, Shrizzioli. After his departure, the club brought over from Philipopolis the active Maccabi athlete Aaron Pardo to replace him.

Early in the year 1913, the Jewish football team joined the Salonika Maccabi Union, and in 1916 Maccabi established a Boy Scouts section and a band. In 1920, because of financial difficulties, it merged with the Zionist association "Theodore Herzl" and in this way formally joined the Zionist Federation of Greece. The merger lasted only until 1928, and, meanwhile, the Maccabi Union, regaining its independence, developed extensive activity for sports events of all kinds. It organized regular calisthenics courses, reorganized its band, which took part in all of the city's Jewish and non-Jewish musical events, created a volleyball section, and captured a distinguished position among the Macedonian soccer teams. Several dozen young boys and girls of the Jewish community also joined the Boy and Girl Scouts (Tzofim and Tzofot). The Maccabi Union also published an annual newsletter in Hebrew and Judeo-Spanish that outlined its activities, and it sent special delegates to the World Maccabi Union congresses. With regard to the founders and most active and prominent leaders of the Salonika Maccabi Union, special mention must be made of the fervent Zionists Solomon Venezia, Isaac David Cohen, and Isaac Shalem, who all immigrated to and settled in Israel.

The "Campbell" Incident

In 1929 the author of this story, as a member of the Community Council of the Jewish community of Salonika, received at his law office an unexpected visit from the editor of a big daily Salonika newspaper.[97] The editor declared openly and without hesitation that if the Jewish community would like to ensure a benevolent attitude of his newspaper toward the Jewish element, it was expected to transfer to him as a donation one of its many building properties. The author of this story thought it his duty to communicate this

---

97 The original manuscript of this article by Asher Moissis includes the full name of this editor and of his newspaper. When he published the article, however, Asher Moissis chose to omit this information.

strange requirement to his Community Council colleagues. All members unanimously rejected it, although they were aware of the possible consequences due to the great influence that the editor's newspaper exercised, on the one hand, on the government party of the great man Eleftherios Venizelos, and, on the other hand, on its readers, who were mostly Greek refugees from Asia Minor and Thrace. Note that, at that time, the Jewish community in Salonika had one of its best Communal Councils, which included president Jacob Gazes, vice president Elias Benousiglio, senator Asher Mallah, deputy Mentesh Benshantzi, dealers Jacques Nahmias, Joseph Bensoussan, and Isaac Amarilio, commerce representative Samuel Botton, and the young lawyer Asher Moissis. In the discussion that followed this tentative communication, the eminent journalist and Greek Parliament member Mentesh Benshantzi noted that if the community submitted to this blackmail attempt, it would whet the appetite of others, thereby subjecting it to consecutive and endless blackmail.

The atmosphere was heavy for the Jews of Salonika at that time for three main reasons:

a. The demographic situation of the city of Salonika had changed as of 1923 with the arrival of over two hundred thousand Greek refugees from Asia Minor and Thrace. The Greek authorities felt naturally obliged to restrict the economic activity of the earlier residents who were mostly Jews.

b. An extreme nationalist organization called Ethniki Enosis Ellas, or "National Union Greece" (EEE), founded then in Salonika by the Greek nationalists and mainly by refugees led an anti-Jewish campaign mainly through the columns of the daily general circulation newspaper *Makedonia*.

c. The Jews of Salonika who had lived for four centuries under Turkish rule and had no political experience had made the mistake of voting continuously, systematically, and with an overwhelming majority during parliamentary and municipal elections in favor of the royal party, the main adversary of the liberal Venizélist party in power.

The newspaper *Makedonia* took advantage of every opportunity to throw poison against the Jewish element by violent articles written mainly by his editor and notorious anti-Semite Nicos Fardis, a refugee himself from the city of Kars in czarist Russia, where he had certainly studied his anti-Semitism.

Under these circumstances, on June 20, 1931, the newspaper *Makedonia* published under a large title the biased information that David Isaac Cohen, a delegate of the Salonika Maccabi to a congress of the World Maccabi Union held in Sofia, participated in a meeting of the Bulgarian Macedonian Revolutionary Committee, where a resolution was passed demanding, among other things, the independence of Yugoslav and Greek Macedonia. The next day the newspaper *Makedonia* returned with a detailed article under a large headline accusing the entire Jewish population of Salonika of supporting and being responsible for this anti-Hellenic attitude of the Salonika Maccabi delegate, adding that Isaac Cohen should not have participated at the meeting of the Bulgarian Revolutionary Organization and, in any event, if present, it was his duty as a Greek citizen to speak, protest, and disassociate himself from the resolution. On June 22, 1931, the same newspaper published a telegram from Athens announcing that the minister of the interior Mr. Lidorikis had confirmed the newspaper's previous information that the Salonika Maccabi Union had participated in anti-Hellenic demonstrations in Sofia.

On that same day and in another column, the newspaper *Makedonia*, in conformance with the Greek law on the press, published the following reply from the Salonika Maccabi Union:

> Mr. Director,
> With reference to your publications yesterday and the day before yesterday that mentioned our organization, we request that under the press law you publish the following and in the same location. It is not true that a representative of our association took part in a Congress of Commitatzis in Sofia. Our association, which is recognized by judicial decision, is a purely athletic body and as such is a member of the Federation of Athletic Associations of Greece. As an athletic association, it is foreign to any political movement that challenges the territorial integrity of the state. In early July 1930, our association sent a letter of greetings to the Congress of the United Maccabi held in Antwerp, Belgium. In his reply

of thanks, the congress president expressed his wishes for our continued collaboration with the World Maccabi Union headquartered in Berlin. The above World Union, on the occasion of sports events organized in Sofia by the Bulgarian Maccabi Union to celebrate the twenty-fifth anniversary of its founding, invited our association to send a delegate to Sofia to meet with its representative, Dr. Rosenfeld, and to discuss with him the terms of our membership. Our association, taking advantage of the departure to Sofia of its member Isaac M. Cohen, tasked him to meet with the representative of the World Union and to discuss with him the possibility of organizing athletic events between all the Maccabi clubs in Balkan countries. We leave it to your readers to judge the discrepancy between all of the above and your publications. But in any case, we cannot leave unchallenged this calumny launched against our association and to which you attribute infernal and insidious activities incompatible with its pure ideals, which are the ideals of the athletic organizations of all countries in the world. Those who know a little history will remember the glory that surrounded the name Maccabi, for which glory we are zealots. Insidious activities such as the ones attributed to us are unworthy of the history of this name, and we reject them with indignation. Our reluctance is even greater seeing this calumny intentionally linked with activities involving the sovereignty of the country of which we are citizens and that loved us as our own mother and that we are ready to defend with our own bodies. Reinforcing this love of country is precisely the deepest objective of our athletic association.

Please receive, etc.

The editors of the *Makedonia* newspaper, ignoring completely this very explicit feedback, continued their campaign aiming to create false impressions and to irritate the public opinion of the Greek population. Thus on June 25, 1931, it published on its front page and under the title "When Maccabi's Guilt Is Clear" another detailed article in which it accused again the leaders of the Maccabi for high treason against the integrity of Greece and accusing as supporting and being jointly responsible the entire Jewish population of the city.

These biased publications of the newspaper *Makedonia* left, as was natural, a great impression on the entire population of Salonika, where the

Jews began to worry seriously and the non-Jews to resent this supposedly unpatriotic attitude of the city's Jews. The governor-general of Salonika, who also held the title of government minister, was in those days the general Stylianos Gonatas, a former prime minister and one of two main leaders of the military revolution of 1922 that followed the military catastrophe of Asia Minor; the great statesman of modern Greece Elefthérios Venizélos was prime minister in Athens. Neither Gonatas nor Venizélos could be considered anti-Semitic, and on the contrary the great Venizélos had on several occasions in the past expressed publicly his liberal and pro-Jewish sentiments. The two boasted of having prominent Jews abroad as best friends, among them the former American ambassador Henry Morgenthau and, in London, the lord Cohen, a fact true and widely known. However, both men and their party in power did not hide their bitterness for the fact that the majority of the Jews of Salonika were their political opponents. It should also be remembered that in Greece political passions were always very acute, and hence a feeling of animosity toward the Jews of Salonika was created in the hearts of all Greeks who belonged to Venizélos' party, animosity exploited by the city's new residents who wanted to get rid of the Jewish element.

The offices of the Jewish community overflowed with Jews reporting incidents that included attacks by irresponsible elements of the Greek population in several Jewish suburbs; calls to police stations requesting their intervention remained without effect. On the other hand, the Greek newspapers in Salonika published statements from Greek national and veterans' associations protesting the "unpatriotic" attitude of the city's Jews. It was clear that the newspaper *Makedonia* and the nationalist organization EEE, in full complicity, fomented an uprising of the Greeks against the Jewish element of the city.

A delegation of the Community Council accompanied by Senator Asher Mallah and Deputy Mentesh Benshanchi visited the minister governor-general Mr. Gonatas to ask him to intervene so that public order would not be disturbed. General Gonatas replied to the delegation that it was difficult for him to control the situation while people were upset and submitted to the community delegates a draft declaration that the Israelite community was to sign and publish in order to help calm spirits. The delegation told him that it would submit the draft to the Community Council, which would be convened immediately. With this text, the community was invited to "disapprove the unpatriotic attitude in Sofia by the delegate of the Salonika Maccabi." The text was written to leave the impression that the Jews of Salonika admitted the truth of the slanderous accusations of the newspaper *Makedonia*, and they tried to lighten the responsibility that weighed upon them. In a most dramatic session of the Community Council, to which several other Jewish personalities of the city were invited and attended, all participants recognized the gravity of the situation and decided to accept in principle the release of the communiqué proposed by Mr. Gonatas, with some small changes to the text, however, so that it did not imply that the community accepted in principle Isaac Cohen's responsibility, especially since until now it had no information on this topic other than what was in the *Makedonia* publications. The amended text highlighted, in any case, that if from the investigation that would follow some fault of the Maccabi delegate during his stay in Sofia was established, "the Jewish community and the entire Jewish population of Salonika would disapprove categorically his attitude and would reiterate their feelings of attachment to the Greek homeland."

It was already midnight when the Community Council proceedings were closed and a delegation composed of the community's vice president Elie Benousiglio, senator Asher Mallah, deputy Mentesh Benshantzi, and the author of this story was charged to go immediately to the home of Mr. Gonatas to submit to him the amended text. The governor-general, warned of the community delegation's presence by the residence doorman, replied that he regretted being unable to receive it. After this response the delegation gave the text to the doorman and walked away, with a very bad premonition. And the result was that the community's communiqué was not published, while on the next day a rumor began to circulate among the members of national and veteran organizations that the community had refused to sign the statement submitted to it by the governor-general to dissociate itself from the accusations against the Jews of the city. Early in the morning, the community delegation visited the government and asked to be received by Mr. Gonatas. The delegation was received by the secretary-general, Mr. Paul

Calligas, who replied that the governor-general had left early for Katerini and would return the next day.

This abrupt departure from his seat at a time of grave emergency for the city that General Gonatas represented in government, a departure that came after his refusal to receive the night before at his residence the communal delegation, was indicative of his true feelings toward the Jewish element and reinforced the premonition of the leaders of the Jewish community that serious activities were being prepared, activities about which the governor wanted to ensure he had an alibi. Faced with this situation, the community sent a "very urgent" telegram to the head of government in Athens, Mr. Venizélos, that read as follows: "JEWISH COMMUNITY SALONIKA HAS INFORMATION FOLLOWING SLANDEROUS AND INFLAMMATORY PUBLICATIONS OF THE NEWSPAPER MAKEDONIA AGAINST THE CITY'S JEWISH ELEMENT, EXTREMIST AND IRRESPONSIBLE ELEMENTS ARE ORGANIZING FOR TONIGHT'S ATTACKS AGAINST THE JEWISH SUBURBS REMOTE FROM THE CITY CENTER STOP. LOCAL AUTHORITIES REFRAIN FROM TAKING NECESSARY MEASURES TO PREVENT EVENT AND CONTROL WELL KNOWN EXTREMIST AND PROVOCATEUR FACTORS STOP. WE SEND YOU AN ULTIMATE CALL TO INTERVENE PERSONALLY AND FORCEFULLY TO PREVENT SERIOUS EVENTS." This telegram remained curiously unanswered, and events unfolded as expected.

That night violent attacks took place against the suburbs inhabited by Jews, and serious and bloody incidents occurred. The attacks were pushed back by the residents of the three Jewish suburbs of No. 6, No. 151, and Baron Hirsch thanks to the defensive measures taken previously by the people who were expecting the attacks and who had set up barbed wire and barricades in some locations. Nevertheless, the attackers had managed to penetrate to the outer parts of suburbs 6 and 151, burning some houses, looting, and wounding some Jewish residents; one of the residents of suburb 151 died of his injuries. The most serious incidents were reported in the Jewish communal suburb farthest from the city, Campbell, where hundreds of Jewish victims of the great fire that ravaged the city of Salonika in August

160

1917 were sheltered. The crowd set fire to the houses, and the suburb was burned in its entirety. Shots were fired during the conflagration against the unfortunate inhabitants, some of whom were injured, and all fled to the center of the city to save their lives. The damage from all these incidents was great, and neither the victims nor the Jewish community received any compensation.

A few weeks after these unfortunate events, the writer was visited at his law office by Messrs. Vourvoulis and Economides, respectively the president of the Association of Reserve Officers of the Greek Army of Macedonia and the president of the Association of NCO Reservists; they told him confidentially that, the day after the incident, Governor-General Mr. Gonatas invited to the governor's office the presidents of all national, veteran, and reservist associations and told them, word-for-word, "The small lesson was a good one, but stop."[98]

Clearly, the Salonika governor-general did not apply in this case the wise Roman principle *gaveant consules* ("may the consuls beware") but rather Virgil's famous line, *claudite jam rivos, pueri sat prata biberunt* ("stop the currents, young men, the meadows have drank sufficiently").

After these incidents the justice of Salonika intervened, and two court cases were opened, one against the journalist Nico Fardis, editor of the newspaper *Makedonia* and author of slanderous and defamatory articles and publications against the Jews and against Cosmides and Haritopoulos, respectively president and secretary-general of the nationalist organization EEE, all three accused as moral instigators of the Greek crowd's uprising. The other case was against the officers of the Maccabi Association of Salonika and against Isaac Cohen, who had represented the club in Sofia and was accused of committing acts against the territorial integrity of the Greek state. The two cases had the following results: after the ordinary investigation, the Salonika Tribunal Court judge Mr. Demetrius Iconomopoulos ordered the three accused Greeks, Fardis, Cosmides and Haritopoulos, to be placed in pretrial custody. This order should, according to the Hellenic criminal procedure code, have been approved by the prosecutor at the Court of First

---

98 In Greek, «καλό ήταν το μαθηματάκι, αλλά σταματήστε».

Instance. The substitute prosecutor Mr. Vellinis, however, spoke against the preventive custody, and according to Greek law and practice, the detention of the accused should have been maintained until the indictment court resolved the disagreement between the two judges. Yet in this special case that does not have a precedent in the annals of Greek justice, the three defendants were released by the police after protests by members of the EEE organization were held outside the Salonika police headquarters. Ultimately, the aforementioned defendants and a few others were referred to the court of the city of Veria at a distance of seventy kilometers from Salonika. The court, after a stormy debate, acquitted the accused Cosmides and Haritopoulos "for lack of sufficient evidence," and the journalist Fardis was qualified as "an idiot who was unaware of his actions"!

On the other hand, the investigation opened against Isaac Cohen and the other leaders of the Maccabi had a much less glorious result. The judge, on the one hand, confiscated the Greek passport of the Maccabi delegate Isaac Cohen to verify his dates of entry to and exit from the territory of Bulgaria. On the other hand, he obtained copies of the official minutes of the Congress of the Bulgarian Macedonian Revolutionary Organization, which included the resolution passed that called for the independence of the Yugoslav and Greek Macedonia. It was then revealed by the two documents and in a formal and irrefutable way that this famous resolution was passed after Isaac Cohen had left the borders of Bulgaria, and therefore he was not present at this congress and had not spoken and had not expressed his approval or his opposition.

After the close of the investigation, the file was forwarded in accordance to the Greek criminal procedure code to the indictment court, which needed to decide whether there were grounds for referring the accused to a competent criminal court. The president of the aforementioned court, Antonios Hamartos, who had followed the tragic events of June 1931, was so surprised and amazed at the revelations that he ordered the presence of the counsel for the EEE organization—the plaintiff—as well as the defendants Isaac Cohen and the leaders of the Maccabi. On the day fixed for the hearing, the counsel for the EEE organization, Menelaos Tsitsouras and Haralampos Sohos on one side and Yomtov Yakoel and Asher Moissis on the other, were present to give the explanation that the three judges of the court had requested. President Hamartos showed to the attorneys Tsitsouras and Sohos Isaac Cohen's passport and the minutes of the "Commitatzis" Congress and asked them if they persisted on the formal charges by their client against the accused. After careful consideration of the aforementioned documents, they gave no response, while the two defense lawyers limited themselves to a smile, a smile full of bitterness and pain. After the lawyers withdrew, the indictment court issued its order, in which it decided that there was no need to refer the accused Jews to the criminal court, and hence they were recognized as fully innocent.

Jews in the Greek Armed Forces: A Short History[99]

E ven though the presence of Jews on the Greek peninsula dates back to pre-Christian Alexandrian times, their military history in the area and their involvement with Greek armed forces was not significant before the Balkan Wars of the years 1912 and 1913. This is because the Jews of the kingdom of Greece were very limited in number and had no military tradition. They were placed under a Greek administration after the Greek War of Independence of 1821, when the Greek state extended only south of Mount Olympus. The considerably more-numerous Jews in the provinces north of Mount Olympus, those in Epirus, Macedonia, and Thrace, continued to live under the Turkish regime until those provinces were annexed to Greece in 1912 and 1913. All of the above, before coming under Greek jurisdiction, lived for about five centuries under a Turkish administration. According to the old Ottoman laws, Jews did not serve in the army, as was also the case with other minorities. When, after the Young Turk Revolution in 1908, compulsory military service was introduced in Turkey, Jews had the right to buy an exemption from military service by paying a specific monetary tax called Bedel.

To systematically examine the military history of the Jews of Greece, we will divide it into the following six periods, which correspond to the general military and combat activity in the country.

1. The period of the wars for Greek independence, between 1821 and 1830.

---

99 This article was first published in Israel in the Hebrew language in 1967 in the journal *Machberet* of the Israeli Defense Ministry, and then a Greek translation appeared in the December 1978 issue of the Greek-Jewish journal *Chronika*. It also appeared in Judeo-Spanish under the title "Jews in the Greek Army" in David Recanati, ed., *Memorial to Salonika*, vol. 1 (Tel Aviv: Committee for the Publication of Books on the Salonika Community, 1971–86).

2. The period of the so-called Macedonian Struggle of the years 1830–1912.
3. The period of the war between Greece and Turkey in 1897.
4. The period of the Balkan Wars in 1912–1923, the First World War in 1914–1918, and Greece's campaign in Asia Minor in 1919–1923.
5. The period of the war between Greece and Italy in 1940–1941 and the Second World War in 1941–1945.
6. The period of the National Resistance during the Italian and German occupation.[100]

1. The Greek War of Independence, 1821–1830

The few Jews who lived in the Peloponnese when the national insurrection of the Greeks against Turkish domination erupted on March 25, 1821, did not participate in this fight. Almost all of the small Jewish population of the revolting Peloponnese was concentrated in Tripolis, capital of the then Turkish *vilayet* of the Morea. The city of Tripolis was put under siege from the first months of the Greek Revolution by the Greeks under the leadership of Theodoros Kolokotronis. Historians of the Greek Revolution only mention one minor episode that took place during the negotiations for the surrender of the city between a delegation of the besieged and the leader of the rebels,

---

100 Notably absent from this list is another armed confrontation that disrupted normal life in Greece for many years: the period of the Greek civil war in 1946–1949. When Asher Moissis wrote this piece, at the height of the Cold War, having an open and balanced discussion of this war was still taboo in Greece (especially during the years of the military dictatorship from 1967 to 1974); hence, presumably, the omission here. Jews fought on both sides of that fratricidal conflict, and, while he did not mention it in this article, Asher Moissis played an active role to protect his coreligionists then. As an example, we quote here an article published by the Jewish News Agency: "ATHENS, May 3, 1950 (JTA) – The Greek government agreed to release five Jews who were condemned to death and 21 Greek Jews imprisoned on a Greek island, provided that they renounce their citizenship and leave for Israel. All of them were convicted by military courts of cooperating with the guerrillas. The negotiations for their release were conducted by Israel representative Asher Moissis with officials of the Greek Ministry of Justice and Foreign Ministry."

Theodoros Kolokotronis. According to these narratives, among the members of the delegation of the besieged who came out of the walls of the city and approached the Greek camp was a Jewish notable of Tripolis named Hanen who, like the other members of the delegation, was armed with a large handgun (*koumpoura*) and a long sword (*yatagani*). Kolokotronis, when he saw the Jew Hanen armed like the other Turks and Albanians, laughed and, after approaching him, removed the gun and the sword, saying "a Jew and a gun and a sword don't match," and he threw these weapons on the ground.

In any case, the Greek struggle for independence was supported enthusiastically by several prominent Jews of Europe, including the Paris journalist Georges Laffitte; Moshe Gaster, the diplomatic representative of the Netherlands in Bucharest, who rescued Prince Ypsilantis, the political leader of the Greek Revolution, from the sentence by the Turks; and the chief rabbi of Westphalia, who conducted sermons in the synagogues and organized fundraisers to support the Greek revolutionaries.

2. Macedonian Struggles, 1830–1912

These liberation struggles were assisted by certain eminent Jews living either in the then free Greek kingdom or in the areas occupied by the Turks. The Larissa doctor David Elia Siakis participated as a military doctor in the activity of the Greek partisans in Macedonia and later joined the regular Greek army as a medical corps officer; he died in Salonika with the grade of major. Also during the invasion of Greek guerillas in Epirus in 1878, the then president of the Jewish community of Yannina David Matatia Levy, also known as Davidson Effendi, a person of great prestige and with great political and social influence with the Ottoman administration, saved numerous Greek prisoners from death by his effective intervention. His intervention was appreciated so much by the government in Athens that he was awarded by King George I of the Greeks the "Silver Cross of the Savior" medal. The same Davidson Levy had earlier received a medal from the Sultan Abdul Hamid, the same medal the sultan had also awarded to Theodor Herzl.[101] Active members of the secret Greek Macedonian Committee were the Jews from

---

101 Asher Moissis married Yeti Levy (my mother), who was Davidson Effendi's granddaughter. Both these medals are in my possession.

Trikala,[102] Iakov Iosif Sides, who served as director of the Trikala Municipal Police, and his brother, Yiuda Iosif Sides or Sidopoulos, along with the one-time president of the Jewish community of Athens, Avraam Konstantinis.

Davidson Levy wearing the two medals awarded to him
by Sultan Abdul Hamid (left) and King Constantine of Greece (right).

3. War Between Greece and Turkey in 1897

In this war, which lasted only a few weeks and resulted in the retreat of the Greek army and the temporary occupation of Thessaly by the Turkish army, around two hundred Jews participated, mainly from Corfu, Zakinthos, Patras, Athens, and Chalkis. It is known that a Jewish soldier from Athens,

---

102 Trikala, which is located in the province of Thessaly in central Greece, is the town where Asher Moissis was born and where he grew up and finished high school before studying law at the National University of Athens.

Elias Isaac Yesuroum, fought and was wounded in the battle of Domokos. Shaul Tchernichovsky,[103] in one of his first literary works, depicts a Jew from Russia who enlisted in the Turkish army as a volunteer as a show of gratitude in anticipation of the assistance that the founder of Zionism, Theodor Herzl, hoped to get from the sultan, Abdul Hamid, for the reestablishment of the Jewish state in the Palestine. This Russian Jew volunteer found himself, according to Tchernichovsky, face-to-face with a Greek Jew defending his adopted country in a battle in Thessaly. It is not clear, however, whether Tchernichovsky wrote this as history or as an allegory. It is also known that, during the temporary military occupation of Thessaly by the Turks, the Turkish authorities imprisoned and tortured the Trikala Jew Raphael Moissis, accusing him of philhellene activity during the period of the Turkish occupation of the city of Trikala. Raphael Moissis was sentenced to be killed by the Turks, but thanks to the intervention of his Turkish friend Küçük Omer Bei, his punishment was "limited" to the cutting off of his left hand.[104]

4. The Balkan Wars in 1912–1923, the First World War in 1914–1918, and Greece's campaign in Asia Minor in 1919–1923

No official statistics are available regarding the number of Jewish officers and soldiers who participated in Greece's wars listed above. Given, however, that prior to the annexation of Epirus, Macedonia, Thrace, and Crete the Jewish population of old Greece was limited to a number not exceeding six thousand individuals, and given the fact that the Jews of Macedonia were not mobilized in the first ten years after they obtained Greek citizenship, we can conclude that the number of Jewish fighters of the aforementioned wars was small and commensurate with the small number of Jews living in the old Greek regions. Thus, the total number of Jews who fought in the Balkan Wars of 1912–13, the first European war of 1914–18, and the Asia Minor campaign of 1919–22 was around four hundred officers and soldiers. To these should be

---

103 Shaul Tchernichovsky (1875–1943) was a Russian Jew born in the Crimea and is considered one of the great Hebrew poets. His nature poetry was greatly influenced by Ancient Greek culture.

104 Raphael Moissis was Asher Moissis' father, and this episode took place two years before Asher's birth in 1899.

added seventy Greek Jews from Egypt who came to Greece during the Balkan Wars and signed up in the Greek army as volunteers. Among them were some nine officers and forty noncommissioned officers. Thirty-two of them were killed in battle, including Daniel Sevilias, a lieutenant from Athens. Moreover, dozens of Jews were injured or killed while on military service or in captivity. We should note, in particular, the excellent military activity of Mordehai Frizis, Avraam Matalon, Isaac Elias, David Siakkis, David Alchanati, and Bohor Siakis, among others. The first two remained in the army as career officers and reached the rank of colonel. Also memorable were the activities of the reserve officer of the Evzones, Daniel Besso from Corfu, and the private Azaria Atoun from Larissa. Their heroic acts were praised by the then commander of the Greek armed forces and king of Greece Constantine as well as the Greek press. Thus, at a meeting in 1913 with the then chief rabbi of Salonika Jacob Meyer, King Constantine said the following: "Israelite soldiers fought in the Greek army as patriots, oftentimes as heroes. During the various battles, the Greek Israelites often fought against other Israelites on the opposite camp. This constitutes clear proof of sincere and true patriotism."

Acts of gallantry and heroism by Jewish soldiers in the Balkan Wars of 1912–13 were also praised by the Greek press at the time. For example, the Athens newspaper *Hellas* described the valor displayed by soldier Azaria Atoun from Larissa, who while fighting in Himarra in Albania in 1913 in the army corps of General Spyromilios was wounded while rescuing the Greek army from a devastating surprise attack. Also, in December 1913, the Athens newspaper *Patris* published a long description full of praise for the heroic actions of the Jewish reserve officer of the Evzones, Daniel Besso from Corfu.[105]

---

105 It is surprising that Asher Moissis failed to mention the recognition of another member of his wife's family, Dr. Nissim Levy, one of Davidson Effendi's sons. Nissim distinguished himself in the medical section of the Greek army during the Balkan Wars of 1912–1913, and the decoration's diploma bears the signatures of King Constantine and Eleftherios Venizélos, the latter as minister of the military. The fact that the two signatures appear side by side gives a particular historical value to the diploma, since disagreement between the two men on Greece's involvement in World War I later divided the entire Greek Nation into Royalists and Venizélists, an enmity that persisted for over two decades.

Also memorable was the participation of Jews from Greece in the First World War and the campaign in Asia Minor. Many Jews were killed or wounded in action during these wars, while many others, among them the rank officer Chaim Sialom Siakis from Larissa, were imprisoned and disappeared in the evacuation of Asia Minor by Greek troops in August 1922.

During this war, moreover, the following individuals served for the first time as senior officers: Mordehai Frizis, Avraam Matalon, David Siakis, Isaac Elias, Iosif Sabetai, and others. Mordehai Frizis served in the First World War as an officer; he also fought and was injured in the Ukraine as a member of the Greek military corps that was sent there with other allies of Greece to fight against the Bolsheviks. Avraam Matalon also participated in these two wars, in Asia Minor serving as a lieutenant colonel at the headquarters of the First Regiment; he was honored with several medals for his distinguished action.

5. The War between Greece and Italy in 1940–1941 and the Second World War in 1941–1945

The Jews of Macedonia, Thrace, and Epirus participated for the first time in the Greek army in these wars. Informal published statistics show that 12,898 Jews were mobilized and fought in these two wars. Officers and reserve officers amounted to 343 and 513 Jews were killed in the Albanian front fighting against the Italians or in the Macedonian front against the Germans. Injured Jews on these two battlefronts numbered 3,743, of which 1,412 bore heavy injuries and became war invalids. Two Macedonian divisions that fought against the Italians in Albania, the Fiftieth and the Sixty-third, where composed primarily of Jews from Salonika and other Macedonian towns. Colonel Mordechai Frizis, who was killed as a true hero in the Battle of Kalamas, is generally regarded as the predominant Jewish military figure of the Greco-Italian war in Albania. Frizis, who served when this war erupted as a regular officer of the Greek army with the rank of lieutenant colonel, had undertaken originally the coordination of the Eighth Division's unit in Delvinaki. After a while, he was appointed commander of a military unit on the front line, which opposed the attacking Italians during nine days of fierce resistance on the southern shore of the Kalamas River in the Vrisohori position. The result was the successful interception of the enemy and the apprehension of the first Italian prisoners of war in Albania. When the Greek general command ordered a counterattack, Mordechai Frizis with the forces under his command succeeded to overturn the opposing superior Italian forces between November 23 and 27, 1940. After crossing the Logaritsas River, he captured a series of fortified hills and the Katzik Bridge. After sequential attacks, he was able to occupy by December 1 the bridge of Premeti on Albanian soil, which was of great military significance. From there he marched up to the Kosovo-Kardamitsi line, where, after a stubborn battle, he forced the Italian troops of the Modena Division to retreat and arrested two hundred more Italian captives. For this achievement and for his gallantry, he was promoted on the battlefield to the rank of colonel. He was killed on the fifth of December in a forward position of the Premeti region. Riding his horse and exposed to the fire of the Italian Air Force, he was encouraging his men to advance. His officers prompted him to dismount and take cover, but he ignored them and was killed by a bomb dropped from an Italian plane. Colonel Mordechai Frizis was, to my knowledge, the only Greek army colonel to be killed in combat during the Greek war in Albania. He was honored with the Gold Medal for Bravery, the War Cross,[106] and other distinctions and medals. The Municipality of Chalcis, his town of origin, erected a bust of Frizis in the city.[107] It should be noted that Mordechai Frizis, when younger, served as president of the Zionist Association of Chalcis, before joining the Greek army as a volunteer.

---

106 In Greek, Χρυσοῦν ἀριστεῖον ἀνδρείας, πολεμικός σταυρός.

107 The statue of Mordechai Frizis in Chalkis was inaugurated by the president of the Greek republic Karolos Papoulias on September 26, 2010.

Mordechai Frizis, hero of the Greek war in Albania.

Mordechai Frizis is widely considered in Greece a hero of the war against Italy; twenty-five streets in different Greek cities, including one in Athens, bear his name.

Other Jewish officers of the Greek army displayed exceptional activity both in the Greek-Italian war and in later military action in Greece. Among these should be mentioned Errikos Nissim Levis of Yannina who was trained in the medical-military School of Athens, promoted to the rank of head physician (colonel), served as director of various military hospitals, and honored with military awards and medals. After surviving the Holocaust and the concentration camps, he returned to Greece and retired with the rank of brigadier.

Colonel Errikos Nissim Levis, here in an earlier picture as a captain.

Also distinguished in the war of 1940–41 was the service of Doctor Jean Alalouf from Salonika. Mobilized by special order of the Greek general staff, he was named an officer and managed one of the military hospitals of Salonika during the war. The regular army major of the medical corps and an expert neurologist, Salvator Sarfatis from Athens, was also particularly appreciated by his superiors for his ethos, his scientific knowledge, and the integrity of his character. After he followed in 1941 the retreating Greek army to Crete, he was arrested there by the Germans and displaced to Auschwitz, where he was killed. With these should be added the permanent officers Joseph Baruch from Corfu and Leo Dostis of Yannina. The former, after fighting as captain of cavalry in the Albanian front, was deported by the Germans to Birkenau where, in September 1944, he organized the well-known armed rebellion of the Greek Jews kept in the Sonderkommando. Leon Dostis, also after fighting in Albania, was sent to retrain in America after the war and was promoted to the rank of major. After resigning from the Greek army, he emigrated in 1953 to Israel and joined the Israeli Defense Forces' tank corps (Tsva Haganah le-Israel) as a major.

The majority of Jews injured and disabled in the Greek-Italian war of Albania were deported in 1943 by the Germans and were killed in Birkenau. A démarche prior to their displacement by the Greek General Confederation of Injured and Disabled War Veterans to the German occupation authorities of Salonika to request their exclusion from deportation did not succeed.

6. The National Resistance during the Italian and German Occupation in 1941–1944

Organized Greek resistance against the forces occupying Greece (Italy, Germany, and Bulgaria) began only at the end of 1942, only a few months before the start of the deportations of the populous Jewish element in Salonika in March 1943. This is most unfortunate; had an organized Greek resistance existed when the deportations started, many thousands of young Jews of Salonika would have escaped to the mountains to join the resistance forces, which would have accepted them willingly. We know this would have been the case based on the fact that when, after the capitulation of Italy in September 1943, German occupation was extended to the Greek provinces south of Mount Olympus, an important portion of the Jewish population of these provinces (especially Thessaly, Chalcis, and Athens) escaped to the mountains and, in cooperation with the resistance forces, avoided displacement and death. The Jews who escaped to the mountains did not form separate Jewish resistance units but joined the active Greek resistance forces. Jewish youth thus joined the Greek resistance forces in the mountainous regions of Vermion in Macedonia and Pelion, Olympus, Hasia, and Pindos in Thessaly. In Athens, too, where many hundreds hid to escape persecution, many cooperated with the resistance and were in contact with Allied intelligence services. The resistance of the Jews in the south of mainland Greece was so good and elaborate that while the German persecutions in this region were ordered by SS General Stroop (the same person who crushed the Warsaw ghetto) on October 8, 1943, the deportations did not take place until March 25, a full six months later, a fact without precedent elsewhere in occupied Europe. As a result, while the surviving Jews in northern Greece were only a small percentage of the Jewish population there, the number of survivors in southern

Greece (especially Athens and Thessaly) was significant. It should be noted that the Jewish Agency in Palestine also contributed to some extent to this result by chartering a special boat that secretly and at regular intervals crossed between the Gulf of Tsakei on the eastern coast of the island of Euboea and the Turkish port of Chesme opposite the island of Chios. This boat carried illegally and at no charge the persecuted Jews and with them many Greek officers from Greece. The passengers traveled from Greece to Turkey and from there continued on to Palestine.

The Germans may not have had as much trouble organizing the deportations elsewhere in occupied Europe as they had in Athens. When General Stroop made the grim order on October 8, 1943, for the Jews of Athens to appear at the synagogue on a certain day to register, nobody obeyed, and he found no Jew there to form the "Council of Elders." He was forced to use agents of the Greek police because the entire Jewish community infrastructure had been dissolved. When, after a few weeks, some Jews began to appear at the synagogue and register, the coordinators of the Jewish resistance (Yomtov Yakoel, Elias Levis, Asher Moissis, and Pepo Iossif) decided to blow up the offices of the Jewish community on Melidoni Street (at the synagogue) where the registration took place, with the objective killing the German SS and their agents and spreading terror to any Jews who considered registering. To this end they came into contact and formed a plan of action with the representative of one of the national resistance networks, the pharmacist Lukas Karamertzanis. The bombing, unfortunately, although well planned, ultimately did not succeed for technical reasons.[108] Thus on March 24, 1944, the Germans surrounded the synagogue and arrested and sent to Auschwitz the eight hundred Jews who had registered.

---

108 It is interesting to note that Asher Moissis is somewhat vague in this public document on the reasons for the failure of the bombing. He was much more specific in his private letter to J. Nehama, which appears earlier in this book. Perhaps he did not want to highlight in public the fact that the resistance forces were only willing to offer their resources and supply of explosives in exchange for cash.

ANCIENT JEWISH EVIDENCE ON THE GREEKNESS OF MACEDONIA

Asher Moissis delivered this speech on May 17, 1964, in Salonika. It made a strong impression and was published in its entirety or in fragments in various newspapers of Athens and Salonika. The sources mentioned in this speech were used a few years ago by researchers on the subject when the issue of the name of the former republic of Yugoslavia was raised. The text, translated into English, was distributed to various international organizations by the Greek diplomatic service and the Central Jewish Council of Greece.

I would like to thank the Society for Macedonian Studies for the honor of being invited here to negotiate from this podium the subject of ancient Jewish evidence on the Greekness of Macedonia. I would also like to thank Professor Fragistas for his kind introduction and all of you for honoring me with your presence here. To reassure you, I warn you that my speech will not last more than fifty minutes.

I thought that this topic, which I plan to negotiate with your indulgence, would be the most appropriate for a speech in the Hall of the Society of Macedonian Studies. The preference for this subject is justified for two reasons: first, because while there remains some occasional and intentional doubt, it is the duty of each historical expert and researcher to proclaim publicly the conclusions of his work; second, because the ancient Jewish references on the subject, having the merit of impartiality and age, constitute an additional argument to refute any alleged claim to the contrary.

Before I refer to the ancient Jewish evidence regarding the Greekness of Macedonia, I need to specify the sources from which I will mine the information.

Ancient Jewish literature has two main sources: the Holy Bible and the Talmud.

By *Holy Bible,* in its narrow sense, we mean the five books of the Pentateuch: Genesis, Exodus, Deuteronomy, Leviticus, and Numbers or Paralipomena.[109] In a broader sense, however, by *Bible* we mean the twenty-four books that include, apart from the Pentateuch, the so-called Hagiographs, namely the Prophets, the Psalms, Ecclesiastes, Solomon's Proverbs, etc.

The Talmud, furthermore, is the voluminous postbiblical text that contains the full record of discussions and interpretations on the Holy Bible conducted by rabbis and rabbinical schools. Given that all this treatment did not have a purely interpretive character but extended to various and countless other materials related to history, geography, sociology, nutrition and health, and even astrology, it is no surprise that the Talmud can assist us in our research.

It is also useful if, as an introduction, a few words are said about the chronology of the authorship of these ancient Jewish sources. And, as far as the date of authorship of the books of the Holy Bible goes, opinions are divided between theologians and free-minded critics. Because the theologians respect the holiness of the texts and are obliged to follow the sacred tradition, they deduce the date of authorship of the holy texts to be those years during which the physical and metaphysical events described are said to have taken place. The scientists, however, freed from traditional beliefs, establish the date of authorship of these biblical texts to be of much later times. In fact, the most daring of these suggest dates as recent as the sixth and fifth centuries BC, or in other words, to the period of the history of the Jewish people after their return from enslavement in Babylon. More specifically, independent researchers date the book of prophesies of Daniel, which I will use as a source later in my speech, to a time after Alexander's campaign in Asia.

Although views regarding the exact age of the Old Testament books are divided, there is agreement as to the creation date of the Talmud. Theologians and scholars agree that its creation started in the second century BC and was completed on the AD fifth century. Thus, its content covers an extensive time period of about seven hundred years.

---

109 Chronicles.

In addition to the ancient Jewish texts of the Bible and the Talmud, which are considered to be holy, ancient Greek literature also contains other nonholy texts. In this category belong primarily the works of the Hellenist Jews of Alexandria, such as the historian Flavius Josephus and the philosopher Philo, the Neoplatonist, along with later works of Jewish philosophers and historians.

It is thus left up to us to scan through these ancient Jewish sources, namely the Old Testament, the Talmud, the Hellenist Jewish writers, and their successors to determine whether and which sources include positions regarding the question that we plan to research.

Evidence in the Bible

From the Old Testament, this main and fundamental source and the primary foundation of Jewish religion and literature, a foundation no less holy and sacred for Christian theology, we find evidence regarding the ancient ethnological character of Macedonia in the book of Prophets Daniel and Joel and in the occult books of the Maccabees.

Chapter 8 of the Jewish text of the prophetic book of Daniel includes the phrase "Ayil Asher Raita, Baal Akarnayim, Malhi Maday, Ou Paras. Veafira A Sair Meleh Yavan."

This fragment was translated by the Seventy as follows:[110] "The ram, which you saw with horns, is the king of the Medes and Persians. And the goat is the king of the Greeks."

According to the theologians, Jewish and Christian, Prophet Daniel is believed to have flourished in the sixth century BC. Consequently, if we consider this version as correct, we have the first testimony for our research, which goes back to a date distant from us by twenty-six full centuries. Free-minded interpreters, on the other hand, place the creation date of the book of Daniel, or at least of the passage above, to a much later age, specifically the second century BC. If one opts for this second opinion, the evidence of interest to us is distant from us by a somewhat shorter period, namely only twenty-two centuries. In any case, it remains beyond doubt that we have in

---

110 The Greek translation of the Seventy reads: *"Ὁ κριός ὅν εἶδες, ὅ ἔχων τά κέρατα, βασιλεύς Μήδων καί Περσῶν. Ὁ τράγος τῶν αἰγῶν, Βασιλεύς Ἑλλήνων"*

front of us a very ancient Jewish testimonial that accepts the Greek character of the region that bears the name *Macedonia*. The content of this evidence is clear and its proof beyond doubt. Because, as is known, those who continue to doubt the Greekness of ancient Macedonia do so while questioning or claiming to themselves the ethnological origins of Alexander the Great.

Since the prophet Daniel in the passage above that described his vision envisioned the future dissolution of the Persian state by the king of the Greeks and this vision was realized in 334 BC by the Macedonian king Alexander, it follows directly that Alexander was recognized as a Greek king and, equivalently, that his Macedonian homeland was recognized since then by the prophet as a Greek land.

As I said, there is no consensus on whether this passage of the prophet was written before or after the Macedonian leader's campaign to Asia. But even if one adopts the minority view and puts into doubt the prophetic element of the book and attributes only a historical narrative to it, this does not weaken the proof: even the most severe critics do not date the creation of the passage to a time later than the second century BC. And this historic document is, for the issue that we are discussing, of special importance for its antiquity as well as for its unbiased and unprejudiced origin. Worth noting is the following detail: the text of the prophet Daniel was preserved to our day in part in the Hebrew language and in part in the Aramaic dialect, which was spoken in Palestine during the Hellenistic times. The passage from the prophecy I presented a few minutes ago, the one containing the vision about the dissolution of the Persian Empire by Meleh Yavan—in other words, by a Greek king—is contained in the portion of the book that is written in the original Hebrew dialect, a fact which reinforces its authenticity and antiquity. We can consequently conclude in all historical consciousness that the Old Testament, through the mouth or, alternatively, though the writings of the prophet Daniel, recognizes Macedonia as a Greek land, the renowned king of that country, Alexander the Great, as a Greek king, and his kingdom as a Greek kingdom.

Reaffirming the prophet Daniel is his colleague the prophet Joel, who, according to Mr. Bartsiotis, honorary professor of the Introduction to the Old Testament at the University of Athens, lived in the ninth or eighth century

BC. Indeed, in chapter 3, paragraph 6 of Joel's Prophesy, we find the following characteristic piece of evidence: "Ou Bene Yehuda Ou Bene Yerushalaim Machartem Lebene Ayavani." In other words, "The children of Judas and the children of Jerusalem you sold to the sons of the Greeks."

Here Joel is said to be prophesying, five or six centuries in advance, the tendency of a certain portion of Israelites to distance themselves from the local customs and traditions and to embrace Greek ones, which took place in Judea at the time of the Epigoni.[111] We will not take a position here on the debate between critics regarding the exact creation date of the prophet's book and whether its content is really prophetic or simply narrative. But even if we adopt the position of those who deny the prophetic character, we are led to accept that, at the latest, by the time of the Epigoni, the Jews recognized those as Greeks and consequently also recognized the land from where they had attacked as being Greek.

Dr. George Box, professor of Old Testament studies at the University of London, insists that a passage of the prophet Habakkuk, who prospered in the seventh century BC, refers to the Macedonian-Greek successors of Alexander the Great. Indeed, chapter B, paragraph 5 of this prophecy includes the vague and difficult to interpret phrase "Ve Af Ki Ayayin Boghed Gherever Yair."[112]

This phrase of the ancient Jewish Masoretic text is so vague and difficult to interpret that, on the one hand, the Seventy translated it metaphorically and almost arbitrarily by the phrase "he who is arrogant and sinful is a man cheering," avoiding altogether to translate the Hebrew word *Yayin*, which means *wine*. The translation of the British Bible Society, in which the man is also said to be rash because of the wine, does interpret correctly, on the one hand, the word *Yayin* as wine but, on the other, leaves the entire passage

---

111 Epigoni or Diadochi (in Greek, επιγονοι, or descendants) refers to the descendants of Alexander the Great.

112 The King James Version of the Bible translates the full paragraph as follows: "Yea also, because he transgresseth by wine, [he is] a proud man, neither keepeth at home, who enlargeth his desire as hell, and [is] as death, and cannot be satisfied, but gathereth unto him all nations, and heapeth unto him all people." In the English Standard Version, it reads, "Moreover, wine is a traitor, an arrogant man who is never at rest. His greed is as wide as Sheol; like death he has never enough. He gathers for himself all nations and collects as his own all peoples."

meaningless. Faced with this difficulty, Professor Box is led to believe that the original Jewish text did not include the word *Yayin*, or *wine*, but the similar word *Yavanim*, which means *Greeks*. Those who accept the opinion of the English professor and theologian would thus find in the prophet Habakkuk yet another piece of evidence that the ancient Jewish sources recognized the Macedonian newcomers, those established in the Middle East, as true and genuine Greeks.

Evidence in the Books of the Maccabees

Jewish tradition does not consider the books of the Maccabees to be part of the "Tanah," or in other words, the twenty-four books of the Old Testament, and this is because their texts were not preserved in Hebrew but only in Greek; for this reason and this reason alone, they are called *Apocrypha* ("hidden"). Nevertheless, according to an announcement made only a few days ago in Jerusalem by the archeologist professor Yigal Yadin, certain ancient Jewish scrolls containing passages of the books of the Maccabees in Hebrew were found during the recent archeological excavations at Herod's ancient palace in Masada of Judea. From this discovery it becomes clear that the so-called Apocrypha books of the Maccabees were originally written in Hebrew, a fact that perhaps will overturn the two-millennia-old Masoretic tradition. But what is of interest to the subject of today's speech is not whether the books of the Maccabees are biblical or Apocrypha but whether they contain a testimony on the issue under investigation. Because, whether biblical or Apocrypha, these were certainly created prior to the second century BC and therefore attest, if they do attest, to our subject.

In the first paragraph in the first book of the Maccabees, we read, "Now it came to pass, after that Alexander the son of Philip the Macedonian, who first reigned in Greece, coming out of the land of Hettim, had overthrown Darius king of the Persians and Medes."[113] Commenting on this passage, we draw the following conclusions. 1. That Alexander of Macedon is recognized

---

113 In the Greek original, «Καί ἐγένετο μετά τό πατάξαι Ἀλέξανδρον τόν Φιλίππου τόν Μακεδόνα, ὅς ἐξῆλθεν ἐκ τῆς γῆς Χεττειείμ καί ἐπάταξε τόν Δαρεῖον Βασιλέα Περσῶν καί Μήδων καί ἐβασίλευσεν ἀντ' αὐτοῦ πρότερος ἐπί τήν Ἑλλάδα».

as king of Greece and 2. That he came out, or in other words, attacked from the land of Hettim. In the Old Testament, specifically in the books of the Chronicles (Numbers) and in Prophet Jeremiah, the Greeks are named in some places *Yavanim* and in other places *Hettiim*. The ancient Jews called *Hettiim* the Greeks from the ancient city of Cition in Cyprus, today's Larnaca. It appears that the Jews had met the Cypriots before coming into contact with the Greek settlers of the Ionian coast of Asia Minor when they were renamed *Yavanim*, which is the plural of *Yavan, Ionian*.[114]

By the way, I note here that, if I needed to also give a speech on the Greekness of Cyprus, I could refer to this confirmatory biblical evidence piece.

Other evidence related to our subject exists in the books of the Maccabees. Thus, paragraph 10 of the first book reads, "And there came out of them a wicked root, Antiochus the Illustrious (Epiphanes), the son of king Antiochus, who had been a hostage at Rome: and he reigned in the hundred and thirty-seventh year of the kingdom of the Greeks."[115]

Also, paragraph 2 of chapter 6 of the same book adds, "And that there was in it a temple, exceedingly rich: and coverings of gold, and breastplates, and shields which king Alexander, son of Philip the Macedonian that reigned first in Greece, had left there."[116]

Evidence in the Talmud

Our research will not turn to delve into the endless pages of the Talmud, the voluminous and very ancient Jewish *"in folio"*[117] that contains almost the entire Jewish knowledge of its time.

The Talmud, narrating the cordial meeting between Alexander the Great and the high priest Simeon the Just upon his entry in Jerusalem in 333 BC,

---

114 Modern Israelis still use the Hebrew word Yavanim to describe Greeks today.

115 In the Greek original, «Καί ἐξῆλθεν ἐξ αὐτῶν ρίζα ἁμαρτωλός, Ἀντίοχος Ἐπιφανής υἱός τοῦ Ἀντιόχου Βασιλέως. Καί ἐβασίλευσεν ἐν ἔτει ἑκατοστῷ καί τριακοστῷ καί ἑβδόμῳ βασιλείας Ἑλλήνων»

116 In the Greek original, «Καί τό ἱερόν ἐν αὐτῇ πλούσιον σφόδρα καί ἐκεῖ καλύμματα χρυσᾶ καί θώρακες καί ὅπλα ἅ κατέλιπεν ἐκεῖ Ἀλέξανδρος ὁ Φιλίππου Βασιλεύς ὁ Μακεδών ὅς ἐβασίλευσε πρῶτος ἐν τοῖς Ἕλλησι»

117 Latin term used in the original Greek text.

calls him "Alexander a Mokdon Meleh Yavan," or in other words, "Alexander of Macedon, King of the Greeks." The Talmud also narrates in the book Seder Ha Dorot ("Genealogical Taxonomy"), with much elegance, the following dialogue between the young and ambitious Greek Hegemon and the Jewish Leader Simon A Zadik ("Simeon the Just"). I translate this dialogue word for word from the Hebrew:

"And Alexander saw that the Temple was grand and most holy in the eyes of the Jews. And he said to himself: 'I will ask the High Priest to place my statue between the hall and the Altar.' And Alexander did as he had thought and said to Simeon the Just: 'If my person graces your eyes, please place my statue between the Temple and the Altar.'

"And Simon the Just replied: 'Our Lord gave us the order that no image and no statue be placed in his Holy Temple. Nevertheless, we will do for you King a deed which will be memorialized forever. Each male child born to the priests, the descendants of the tribe of Levi on this year, will take your own name, Alexander.'

"And so the name Alexander was introduced in Israel in his memory from generation to generation."

Indeed, in Jewish onomatology,[118] which is so religiously strict, ever since that time the name Alexander was added to the list as a Jewish name, it could be found not only among the Hellenistic Jews of antiquity but also among later Jews and indeed among some of the contemporary Jews of Greece.[119]

And the reference above is not the only Talmudic one of the Macedonians who established themselves in the Middle East as a Greek race. Chapter 11 of the book Megillat Ta'anit ("Scroll of Fasts")[120] reads, "Vayishlah Gaskalgas Meleh Yavan Tzelamin Lamid Bemikdash Adonai" ("And Gaskalgas King of the Greeks sent images to be placed in the Temple of the Lord").

---

118 The proper classification of names—Asher Moissis wrote a book on the subject of Greek-Jewish onomatology.

119 Translator's note (Alexander Moissis): I can personally attest to this fact...

120 The Megillat Taanit is a very early (AD first century) list of memorable days in Jewish history.

We do not know, of course, which Greek king by the name of Gaskalgas the Talmudic text implies, but what is of interest to us is that it recognizes him as a Greek.

The second chapter of the same book includes the phrase "Vayiben Ghedoud Ayavanim Anil Chamim Im Bene Israel Ish Echad Ousmmo Nicano" ("And among the Greeks fighting the children of Israel was a certain man named Nicanor").

We know from that time's history that one of the generals of the Seleucid king Antiochus the Epiphanes, who was sent to the land of Israel with the order to destroy the Jewish religion and to replace it with idolatry, was named Nicanor.

I could also call upon and quote a multitude of other passages of the Talmudic texts in which Alexander as well as the Epigoni ("descendants") Seleucids and Ptolemies are recognized as Greek and their Macedonian birthplace as a Greek land. Of special importance, however, is the fact that in most of the cases where Alexander is mentioned, he is referred to in Hebrew as "Alexander A Mokdon Meleh Yavan," or "Alexander of Macedon, King of Greece."

Evidence in the Works of Flavius Josephus

I will now leave the Talmud to bring before you other converging Jewish evidence included in the preserved text of the famous Jewish Hellenist writer of the AD first century, Flavius Josephus, or, in Hebrew, Yosseph Ben Matatia, or Joseph the son of Matathias. This Jewish historian authored three works, namely the *Antiquities of the Jews*, *Jewish War*, and the apologetic work *Against Apion, or on the Antiquity of the Jews*.

If one researched the texts above, he or she would be led to the conclusion that Joseph, whenever he has the opportunity to refer to the Greeks or the Macedonians and to Greece or Macedonia, makes no distinction between the names and alternates between them, considering the Macedonians to be Greeks and the Greeks to be Macedonians.

I will illustrate a few of the very many such pieces of evidence that I compiled from the work *Antiquities of the Jews* that prove the validity of my historical conclusion. Here they are:

Book 11 #337: "And when the Book of Daniel was showed him wherein Daniel declared that one of the Greeks should destroy the empire of the Persians..." Thus Joseph here, while narrating the presentation by the high priest of the book of the prophet Daniel to Alexander the Great upon his entry in Jerusalem in 333 BC, where he prophesied, as I mentioned earlier, the destruction of the Persian Empire by a Greek king, he also recognizes Alexander as a Greek.

Book 8 #61: "Solomon began to build the temple in the fourth year of his reign, on the second month, which the Macedonians call *Artemisius,* and the Hebrews *Jur.*" Here Joseph names the Greeks as Macedonians.

Book 8 #95: "He also placed a partition round about the temple, which in our tongue we call *Gison,* but it is called *Thrigcos* by the Greeks." As we can see, on this occasion the Jewish historian uses the term *Greeks* instead of the synonym *Macedonians.*

Here are a few other passages from the same text that attest to the fact that the words *Greeks* and *Macedonians* are used as synonyms.

Book 8 #100: "and when this invitation of the whole body of the people to come to Jerusalem was everywhere carried abroad, it was the seventh month before they came together; which month is by our countrymen called *Thisri,* but by the Macedonians *Hyperberetoets.*"

Book 8 #154: "When he had therefore built this city, and encompassed it with very strong walls, he gave it the name of Tadmor, and that is the name it is still called by at this day among the Syrians, but the Greeks name it Palmyra."

Book 11 #109: "And as the feast of unleavened bread was at hand, in the first month, which, according to the Macedonians, is called Xanthicus, but according to us Nisan, all the people ran together out of the villages to the city..."

Book 8 #312: "Now it was in the thirtieth year of the reign of Asa that Omri reigned for twelve years; six of these years he reigned in the city Tirzah, and the rest in the city called Semareon, but named by the Greeks Samaria."

Book 11 #148: "those that were of the tribes of Judah and Benjamin came together on the twenty third day of the ninth month, which, according to the Hebrews, is called Tebeth, and according to the Macedonians, Apelleius."

Book 10 #273: "that the he-goat signified that one should come and reign from the Greeks, who should twice fight with the Persian, and overcome him in battle, and should receive his entire dominion."

Book 11 #286: "on the twenty-third day of the twelfth month, which we call Adar, but the Macedonians called Dystrus."

Book 11 #184: "After the death of Xerxes, the kingdom came to be transferred to his son Cyrus, whom the Greeks called Artaxerxes."

Book 12 #322: "And this desolation came to pass according to the prophecy of Daniel, which was given four hundred and eight years before; for he declared that the Macedonians would dissolve that worship."

We observe that, while on line 273 of book 10 Josephus, while referring to the prophet of Daniel, calls the person who is bound to dissolve the Persian state a Greek, here, while referring to the same prophecy, calls him a Macedonian. This is due to the fact that, as we said earlier, in Josephus's mind the two ethnological and geographic words are equivalent and synonymous.

We will leave Josephus after we quote yet another passage of his antiquities, the one from book 12 #414, which offers us another historical testimonial related to our conclusion.

Book 12 #414 reads, "And when he was dead, the people bestowed the high priesthood on Judas; who hearing of the power of the Romans, and that they had conquered in war Galatia, and Iberia, and Carthage, and Libya; and that, besides these, they had subdued Greece, and their kings, Perseus, and Philip, and Antiochus the Great also; he resolved to enter into a league of friendship with them."

Perseus, as is known, was king of Macedonia and flourished during the first half of the second century BC and was son of Philip the Fifth, whom he succeeded on the royal throne in 178 BC. When describing the occupation of the Greek region, the Jewish historian includes these Macedonian kings along with the Great Antiochus, considering Macedonia to be a Greek province.

Evidence in the Works of Philo of Alexandria

This is the data I mined by researching the texts of Josephus.[121] I also searched through the discourses of the other and almost-contemporary Hellenistic author, the Neoplatonist philosopher Philo of Alexandria, about whom the ancients made the following well-known statement: "Either Philo is platonizing or Plato is philonizing." Philo, however, was not a historian, and his works, dedicated to philosophical theology and metaphysics, did not, of course, give him the opportunity to leave us with much historical evidence on the subject of interest to us now. However, whenever Philo had the opportunity in his philosophical studies to imply the Greek origin of the Macedonians, he did so openly, either by distinguishing the total of the Greeks from the barbarians or by naming specifically the Macedonians and their king Alexander as Greeks.

Thus, in his philosophical work *On the Fact that Everything Wonderful is Free*,[122] referring to Alexander's attempt to force the Indian gymnosophist Kalanos[123] to move with him to Greece, he says the following: "Alexander the Macedon wishing to demonstrate to Greece the wisdom of the Barbarians... invited Kalanos to move with him...And as he was not convincing him, he told him that he 'will be forced to follow.' To which he (Kalanos) smartly and politely replied: 'How are you going to present me as a worthy man to the Greeks, Alexander, when I will have been forced to do something against my will?'"

Evidence in the Itinerary of Benjamin of Tudela

After this reference, I continue my course to other evidence of my coreligious ancestors, and first, I will call upon a passage of the *Itinerary* of the famous Spanish Jew the rabbi Benjamin of Tudela. This wealthy rabbi of Navarre, who could be described as the pioneer of modern travelogues, set

---

121 Now that these texts can be found in digitized form on the World Wide Web, such a word search takes only a few minutes. Yet, in 1964, it would have taken Asher Moissis many hours to compile this list...

122 Philo: Quod deus sit immutabilis, or The Unchangeableness of God, also referred to as Free Will.

123 Also referred to as Calanus, Calanos, Kalyanaswami.

out in AD 1164 from the small town of Tudela in Spain to visit and get to know the Jewish communities of the Balkans and the Middle East. After arriving in Corfu, which was then part of the kingdom of Sicily, he crossed to Árta and continued his tour through all of southern and northern Greece and the islands of the Greek archipelago. In his *Itinerary*, which he wrote in Hebrew, the rabbi Benjamin writes the following about his impressions after setting foot on Greek soil: "from there (in other words, from Corfu), after a two-day journey by sea to Árta, which is where the kingdom of Manuel, the land of the Greeks, begins." Later, after describing his itinerary through Stereá Ellás, the Peloponnese, and Thessaly, he notes the following: "and from there on, after a journey of two days, we arrive in the city of Salonika, which was founded by Seleucus, one of the four kings of Greece who ruled after Alexander..."

We will forgive, of course, the itinerant rabbi the historical inaccuracy regarding the true founder of Salonika[124] and focus only on the elements related to our topic. First he narrates that from Árta starts the kingdom of Manuel, the land of the Greeks. But, at the time when Tudela passed through Árta and then visited Salonika, the king of Byzantium was Manuel I Komnenos, who ruled from AD 1143 to 1180. In this kingdom, which had Constantinople as its capital, belonged all of Macedonia, which is therefore recognized as Greek by Tudela, since he tells us that the kingdom of Manuel, the land of the Greeks, starts in Árta. Rabbi Benjamin repeats this recognition of Macedonia as a Greek land by adding that Salonika was founded by Seleucus, one of the four kings of Greece, who ruled after Alexander, thereby characterizing the Epigoni or descendants of Alexander as Greek kings.

Evidence in the Works of Maimonides

Another Jew contemporary to Tudela, also a rabbi, though much more famous in Jewish and world history, Moses-ben-Maimon, who Hellenized his name to Maimonides, also left us a valid historical stamp regarding the Greekness of the land on which we stand today. Maimonides was born in

---

124 The city was founded by the king Cassander of Macedon around 315 BC and was named after his wife Thessalonike, a half sister of Alexander the Great and daughter of Philip.

Córdoba in Spain in AD 1135 and died in Tiberias of Israel in 1204. He was the unique Jewish philosopher of the Middle Ages who enriched Jewish thinking with the teachings of Aristotelian philosophy. In his book *More Nevouchim* (The Guide for the Perplexed), Maimonides, as he prefaces his work and introduces to his readers Aristotle, the Macedonian philosopher from Stageira, refers to him as Greek and declares him one of the best-known representatives of the ancient Greek culture. This culture, according to Maimonides, thanks to the conquest of Asia by the Greco-Macedonian royal dynasty, was also transplanted to Judea and contributed to the cross-pollination between Hellenism and Judaism and to the creation of a new philosophical and religious combination that opened new paths and gave new directions to human civilization.

Evidence Based on Archaeological Findings in Macedonia

Other additional documents and monuments could be considered as old and authentic Jewish evidence of the Greekness of Macedonia. Among them one can quote the following: Lazaros Velelis, professor of Judaic studies at the University of Salonika, found a few years ago in Kastoria a very old medieval copy of the Old Testament written in Greek but with Hebrew characters. The Jews of Kastoria spoke Greek, as was the case for those in Salonika and all the other cities on the Greek peninsula since Hellenistic times and until the populous arrival of Jewish refugees from Spain in the AD fifteenth century. Since many of them, however, despite the fact that Greek was their mother tongue, did not know how to write in Greek but knew how to read and write in Hebrew, they needed to read the Bible in Greek but written using the letters of the Hebrew alphabet. This Greek-Jewish copy of the Bible was bought about thirty-five years ago by the then newly founded University of Salonika and is now located in the university library, having been rescued from certain destruction during the racial persecutions.

Also, at the old Jewish cemetery of Salonika, tombstones were found and uncovered that bear inscriptions written in Greek and Hebrew going back to Hellenistic and medieval dates. The relevance of these documents and memorials to the subject of our research may be indirect, but they are no less valuable and reliable. The fact that the old Jewish residents of Macedonia wrote their holy books using Hebrew characters but in the Greek language and carved Hebrew and Greek inscriptions on their tombstones means that they were linguistically assimilated to their environment and that this environment was consequently a Greek one. If this environment had been, say, a Slavic one, then the tombstones would have been Judeo-Slavic and the holy Jewish books would have been written in Hebrew letters but in a Slavic language. This argument is enhanced *mutatis mutandis*[125] by the fact that in other countries, such as Egypt and ancient Mesopotamia, old Bibles and old tombstone inscriptions were found written in Hebrew and Arabic, attesting not only to the influence but also the ethnological character of the environment.

As indicative of the position that Jewish thinking takes on our topic of research, we can take the opinion expressed by Heinrich Graetz, the most authoritative of modern Jewish historians, in his erudite eleven-volume *History of the Jews*. Graetz, who lived about a century ago, was professor of Jewish history at the University of Breslau and could be parallelized with the Paparrigopoulos of Greek history. This Jewish history expert declares openly that ancient Macedonia was a Greek country; that its king Alexander changed the course of human history with his conquest of Asia; that its royal dynasty was also Greek; and that the cultural and demographical composition was Greek, even though, as in any other province, other racial elements were also present in Macedonia. In his entire erudite work, whenever Graetz has the opportunity to refer to the activities of the successors of Alexander the Great in Asia and in Egypt, he refers to them as Greek-Macedonians, their customs as Greek customs, their religion as a Greek religion, and their behavior in general as Greek behavior, in contrast to its opposite, barbaric behavior.

These are, as far as I know, the ancient Jewish pieces of evidence that testify on the subject of my speech. Clearly others could be added to these, if I knew and had researched the sources further.

---

125 "By changing those things which need to be changed," or more simply, "the necessary changes having been made." The Latin words are used in the original Greek text. This term is used frequently in law, philosophy, and logic to parameterize a statement with a new term.

But if history in itself offers us the evidence that I presented, another related science, the philosophy of history, offers us additional and equally valid certificates. And this science, without the study of which the dry historical narrative and simple quoting of events cannot be didactic, confirms our conclusions. The philosophy of history teaches that, for the creation of a historical unity between a country and a people and the legalization of historic claims of a people on a country, the simple and symptomatic right of occupation of that country or its simple transit by foreign ethnic elements does not suffice. It is additionally required that the occupying people connect with the land and with all those necessary bonds and forges all the necessary links that are described in one word as "civilization." Under the spectrum of this teaching, if we examine the history of Macedonia during the last twenty centuries, we will observe that however many people crossed it and authorities ruled upon it, for however long, none became attached to Macedonia with as clear and as unambiguous cultural ties as the ones with which the Greeks became associated with this land. And irrefutable witnesses for this conclusion are not only the discoveries brought to light constantly by archaeologists but also the living monuments of art, literature, and other expressions of the human spirit that constitute the historical and cultural past of Macedonia.

And thus the ancient Jewish sources that I was able to collect and quote to you in today's speech are in full harmony with these teachings and conclusions.

And if we would like to validate these sources and these conclusions with the human activity currently under way in all fields in Macedonia and in its beautiful capital, activity that indicates great and perhaps unprecedented progress, we will find the opportunity to apply the saying of the Greek epigrammatic philosopher Menander, who said, "Time discovers truth."[126]

---

126 In Greek, "ἄγει πρός φῶς τήν ἀλήθειαν, χρόνος"

GREECE'S SYSTEM OF GOVERNMENT IMPEDES
ITS PROSPERITY AND PROGRESS

The following letter was written by Asher Moissis in January 1968, yet continues to be relevant today. The text illustrates that Greece's governance system has been a persistent issue that has yet to be addressed at its core. Asher Moissis discussed this letter with the junta's vice president Stylianos Pattakos after the military coup that dissolved democracy and brought to power the dictatorship of the colonels. Upon assuming power (and after imprisoning many of the country's democratically elected leaders), the junta declared that their objective was to restore order, rewrite the constitution, and quickly return the country to democracy. The credibility of their claim diminished as the months and then years of the seven-year dictatorship passed. The fact that, a few months after the military coup, Asher Moissis was willing to present his framework on what he considered to be the proper operation of a free democracy suggests that while he was, like many other Greeks at the time, frustrated by the country's political impasse in the midsixties, he was willing to give the benefit of the doubt to the military dictators in the first few months of their reign and to believe their claim that they were planning to revise the constitution and to call for free elections soon thereafter. Some would consider his position to be overly optimistic but sincere; others would describe it as naive and may condemn it. In any case, the episode illustrates that he had the courage and the prestige to engage in a dialogue with and to lecture the military dictators on the proper operation of a free democracy. And, whether one likes it or not, the dictators were, at least early in their reign, willing to listen.

In the text that follows, I record my personal thoughts that stem from my legal studies, my observations on Greek public life, and the comparative study of constitutional institutions in other countries and most notably in Israel.

These conclusions may be summarized in general terms as follows:

1. General Observations

Almost all observers of public life in modern Greece recognize that the Greek state infrastructure is not functioning smoothly. Some of these observers blame this problem on the ruling class, which they accuse of not fulfilling its required role and not using its influence to correct the problems. Others, on the contrary, attribute the misfortune to the Greek masses, blaming them for lacking political maturity and being inspired by individualistic attitudes that prevent them from making sacrifices for the general interest and the needs of collective life.

I reject both explanations, despite the fact that I agree that the Greek state infrastructure suffers at its core.

I was born and lived for over half a century within the Greek environment; I also traveled extensively and studied foreign institutions and the characteristics of other peoples and the Israeli people in particular. Based on these, I can ascertain that the Greek people are not in general terms much different from other people who thrive and prosper. I would dare to add that Greece, with its national attributes and the climate under which it lives, would lead in prosperity and progress if it was not impeded by the break that slows it down and prevents it to develop and to exploit the advantages of its race and Greek climate. And this break is nothing else, in my opinion, but the country's bad and unfortunate system of government.

2. The Weaknesses of the Current System

The basic and main weaknesses of the current system of government are the following:

    a. **The pressing, unconstrained, and unhealthy dependence of the rulers on those they govern.** A product of this ill and constraining dependence was the glorified and genuinely Greek symptom of the "political exchange." On the one hand, this symptom transformed the parliamentary representatives of the Greek nation, who lacked neither patriotism nor skills, to weight-bearing dispatchers of the most improbable petty issues and petty interests of the voters and party leaders; on the other hand, it removed from the members of the government and parliament the opportunity to focus their attention and interest on the care of the country's general affairs.

b. **The professional parliamentarians.** The pressing, uncon-
strained, and unhealthy dependence of members of parliament
on the voters has led over time to a reduction in the number
of those actively involved in politics, and to the development
of professional parliamentarians. This symptom is, from the
Greek point of view, truly discouraging. No other country in
the Balkans has as many distinguished scientists and other spe-
cialists as Greece. Athens, in particular, has a larger proportional number of leading scientists and industrialists relative to
the capital cities of neighboring countries. Nevertheless, these
distinguished individuals, as a rule, do not become involved in
politics and do not run for public office due to the real danger
of compromising their persons in the current system of election
of public representatives to parliament. In Greece it has become
common knowledge that those elected are in their majority not
the distinguished[127] ones. This weakness needs to be lifted from
within in the most radical way. This can be achieved via the following two constitutional amendments:

1. The elimination of the division of the country into multiple
    electoral districts and the establishment of a single electoral
    district for the entire country and
2. Term limits so that individuals who have served for more than
    two prior consecutive terms are not allowed to be candidates for
    parliament.
    I discuss each of these constitutional amendments and their
    expected results in more detail below.

3. Single Electoral District

The country's division into multiple and more or less narrow electoral districts brought, in my opinion, many ills to Greek public life and influenced

---

127 To emphasize his point in the original Greek text, Asher Moissis elegantly chose
the similar words εκλεγομενοι (eklegomeni, or elected) and εκλεκτοι (eklekti, or distinguished). The English word eclectic originates from this Greek word εκλεκτοι but
has taken the meaning of assorted rather than distinguished in the English language.

negatively the country's fate. This division was the cause for the development of localism and encouraged citizens to seek the satisfaction of their personal interests at the expense of the interests of the whole.

Aristotle, in his *Politics*, recognizing this poor institution, induced "the *many* are more incorruptible than the *few*; they are like the greater quantity of *water* which is less easily corrupted than a little."[128]Even though this wise maxim was written by a Greek in the Greek language, it did not, unfortunately, serve to guide the kindhearted Greek citizen. Ever since the declaration of Greek independence, Greek citizens were not trained to place, via their basic institutions, the well-being of the state above their own persons.

The system of the single electoral district, which has been in effect in Israel since the reestablishment of the Jewish state, has produced excellent results and is considered by many as one of the key reasons for the prosperity, the progress, the cohesion, and the unmatched development of its value-producing capabilities. If transplanted to Greece, this system will actively address many problems; more specifically, it will free the parliament deputies from the tribute tax to the voter, since they will be elected by all Greek voters. Voters will know them only from their interventions in parliament, their studies, their recommended legislation, their articles, and in general from events of public nature. This will help the deputies to focus their time and attention on the study of legislation, the budget, and the general issues facing the country instead of being the weight-bearing dispatchers of the selfish demands of a small group of voters. It will allow the inert and hibernating distinguished individuals of Greek public thought and industry to enter the political arena and to offer their capabilities to the nation. It will free significantly the administration from the pressing intervention of deputies and will allow it to complete its business in an unbiased fashion and within the spirit of the laws.

4. Professional Parliamentarians

The introduction of parliamentary term limits would restore health to future public life in Greece. This institution, new in its kind, if applied to

---

128 "Ὡς τό ὕδωρ τό πλεῖον, οὕτω καί τό πολύ (τῶν ἀνθρώπων), τῶν ὀλίγων ἀδιαφθορώτερο"

the Greek Constitution that is currently being reformed, will have, among others, the following positive impact on Greek public life:

a. It will put an end to the monopolization of the post of deputy by a small number of politicians;

b. it will raise the position of deputy in the public mind; and

c. it will automatically render possible the occasional renewal of the elements of public life and the ongoing transfusion of new blood in the body of the Greek parliament, since its individuals who have served two consecutive terms will not be allowed to be candidates in the parliamentary elections that immediately follow these two terms.

An exception to this limitation should be introduced for parliamentary prime ministers and the heads of parties legally recognized by the state and the constitution,[129]and this should be done so that continuity is secured in the leadership of the country.

5.   The Electoral System

While it is commonly recognized that the system of simple majority is the fairest of all, nevertheless this system was not established in Greece by the constitution, but how it was to be applied at each point in time was left up to the law to determine. This flexibility would have been justified by the fear that transient popular currents bring to power authoritarian and not truly democratic parties. Nevertheless, I believe that this danger can be removed effectively by

a. the establishment of a single electoral district;

b. regulating the organization and controlling the operations and activities of the country's political parties; and

c. prohibiting via the constitution the collaboration between parties in election campaigns.

---

129 The language used here by Asher Moissis to describe political parties is indicative of that used during the period that followed the Greek Civil War, when the Communist Party and its leadership were outlawed.

Consequently, the only occasion for the assumption of political power by means of elections of a certain party representing an illiberal ideology[130] would be in the case that the illiberal party would

a. achieve its recognition by the Constitutional Court as a legal party, which would be impossible and
b. would also succeed in gathering the absolute majority of votes via misleading the public, which is also highly unlikely.

In any case, and as a safety valve, a clause could be added to the constitution by which the simple majority electoral system could be converted to another system by a vote of two-thirds of the total number of the members of parliament and only after a motion by the Constitutional Court.

However, the introduction of the single electoral district is not sufficient to remove the unhealthy dependence of the deputy on the voters. It is necessary that the damaging system of named ballots, which is ultimately responsible for the system of political favors, also be removed forever. Political parties recognized by the Constitutional Court should participate in the parliamentary elections based on the content of their political programs; these political programs, in their initial or modified content, should be reviewed by the Constitutional Court; and the list of candidates for parliamentary posts should be proposed by the collective leadership of each party. The relative order of priority of the candidates should be established by the party's collective leadership so that if, for example, the party elects fifty members to seats in parliament, the first fifty individuals on the list would be appointed.

Especially in Greece, this operation is necessary to revitalize the parliamentary system. Greek voters should be limited to the right to express by their votes their preferences for the party whose officially registered political program they approve and for the party candidates based on their awareness of the prioritized list established by the party leadership.

---

130 Clearly, the Communist Party is being suggested in this section.

In order to prevent the transfer of the selection of individual candidates to a handful of party leaders after removing it from the voters, I consider it useful that the lists of candidates and their order of priority be composed via a public session of the general assembly of the party and formally submitted to the Constitutional Court. This will establish the system of selecting candidates by a college of electors who, after establishing the list of candidates, would relinquish their duties and would not hold under their influence the elected deputies.

The system described above is the one current in Israel today in a somewhat improved form.

6. Organization of Political Parties

The organization and operation of political parties has not benefited to date from regulatory coverage from the constitution and the laws. Thus, an inherently important issue that influences greatly the fate of the Greek nation has been left to date unregulated with dire consequences. The fact that certain guidelines have not been set in the organization and operation of political parties constitutes today a misunderstanding of the concept of democratic governance. After all, according to one constitutional theory, parties are the source and expression of political power, in lieu of the people. Just as it is not antidemocratic to have laws regulate the establishment and operations of a simple association or partnership as a private law entity, all the more it is not antidemocratic to specify a constitutional and legislative framework for the organization and operation of the country's political parties, which are inherently public law entities. Attention, of course, will need to be paid so that this framework is not so tight as to become reactionary and prevent the free development and implementation of new political, social, and economic currents that interfere with the core ideas of freedom and true democracy. When a river or a stream threatens during times of flood to leave its natural banks, to inundate the plains and to cause damage, for the welfare of the community and the preservation of the common good, it is essential that levees and dykes be built or even that the natural bank of the river or stream be modified. This should be done under the condition, of course, that the intervention does not extend to the full restriction of the flow of the water, in which case the disaster would be greater.

In the context of these thoughts, the following constitutional measures would be recommended:

a. Political parties should become associated with an ideology and cease being tied to an individual. To this effect:

b. A political party can be founded by a minimum of one thousand Greek voters meeting in a public assembly.

c. The administration of each political party needs to consist of multiple members and certainly not fewer than fifteen individuals.

d. The political party should always be represented by this multimember board.

e. Each political party needs to have written bylaws where the program and goals of the party are described clearly and in detail.

f. The bylaws must describe the mechanism for calling a general assembly and for the election by the assembly of the board of directors.

g. The bylaws also need to include an explicit statement that the execution of the party's program and general objectives will be pursued solely through the persuasion and education of the people and that the use of force, misleading propaganda, and illegal means will be prohibited.

h. The bylaws of each political party should be submitted for approval to the Constitutional Court. The party becomes a legal entity as a political organization only after publication of the approval of the bylaws by the court.

i. The Constitutional Court approves the bylaws if their contents are consistent with the constitution and laws in force.

j. Only officially recognized political parties are allowed to participate in parliamentary elections and the country's public life.

k. The Constitutional Court has the right to audit the finances of political parties and to decide and justify a particular party's dissolution if convinced that the party (i.) violated the constitution, the laws, or its own bylaws; (ii) diverged extensively from its stated objectives; (iii) utilized covert funds; (iv) its representatives were condemned by a criminal court for violation of the articles of the Penal Code or for violating the rule that the execution of the party's program and general objectives will be pursued solely through the persuasion and education of the people and without the use, attempted use, or promotion of force; (v) failed to participate in two consecutive parliamentary elections.

7. Funding of Political Parties

Officially recognized political parties are funded by the Public Treasury with amounts determined by the current Constitutional Court. The property of a party that is dissolved by a decision of its general assembly or by the Constitutional Court returns to the state.

8. Constitutional Court

The Constitutional Court, based in Athens, consists of all life-tenured members of the Council of the State[131] and the Supreme Court[132] and is presided over in rotating two-year terms by the president of the Council of the State and the president of the Supreme Court, starting with the former.

By royal order and a proposal by the Constitutional Court, a commissioner of the Constitutional Court is appointed among the life-tenured members of the Council of State and the Supreme Court. Details on the operations of the Constitutional Court and its commissioner are determined by a regulation voted on by the court and approved by royal order; changes to the operations would follow the same approval process.

9. Jurisdiction of the Constitutional Court

Under the jurisdiction of the Constitutional Court are the following:

a. The oversight of the organization and operation of the country's political parties and the conduct of elections.

---

131 In Greek, Συμβουλίον τῆς Ἐπικρατείας.
132 Greece's supreme court is called the Areus Pagus.

b. The trial of objections against the validity of parliamentary elections.

c. The joint exercise of royal prerogative toward dissolving the parliament.

d. The trial of suits against members of the State Council and the Supreme Court as well as disciplinary power exercisable on them.

e. The submission of recommendations to the king and parliament on necessary reforms to the constitution and the laws.

f. The exercise of other authorities as described by relevant laws.

10. Parliament

The total number of deputies should not exceed two hundred.[133]Deputies enjoy immunity only during parliamentary sessions.

Parliamentary compensation should not be determined, as has been the case in the past, only by a decision of the parliament but with the joint approval of the Constitutional Court.

The privilege of free transportation of deputies within the country by any means of transportation should be abolished or limited so that half the cost is covered by the deputies themselves. Equivalently, their privilege to free postal and telegraphic service should also be abolished as it can lead to abuse.

Parliamentary discussions on questions and on proposed laws should be determined in such a way as to avoid pointless and demagogic excesses. The most relevant system for deliberations, in my opinion, is the one in power at the Israeli Knesset. According to this system, prior to every discussion related to a general question or an important law, the president of parliament, in conjunction with the head of government and the leaders of the parliamentary parties, determines the maximum time allotted to the discussion. This time is distributed among the political parties in proportion to their share of seats. Each party's leadership then distributes among its presenters the time allotted to the party.

Parliament can only be dissolved by the king and only after the joint opinion of the Constitutional Court.

---

133 The total number of deputies then and still today is three hundred.

11. Plebiscite

I believe that Greek voters have matured so that they may be recognized the right to express their opinion via plebiscite on necessary amendments to the constitution and on other important governance issues that may arise.

So that the institution of the plebiscite is not abused, this should be proclaimed by the head of state and only after the agreement of parliament and the Constitutional Court.

A plebiscite called under the restrictions described above could be used to modify fundamental and nonfundamental clauses of the constitution but not simple legislative rather than constitutional clauses.

I thought it useful to record the above thoughts as a general outline, and if they are considered to be worthy of further attention, I will be happy to extend them and to express them in the appropriate legal terms.

Asher Moissis in a conversation with Menachem Begin in the early 1970s. Begin was then head of the opposition and in 1977 became prime minister of Israel. Throughout his active life, while living in Greece, Moissis maintained regular communication with the leaders of Zionism and later of the Jewish state and closely followed political developments in Israel.

INDEX

15266628R10128

Made in the USA
Charleston, SC
26 October 2012